Building Your Business

Marketing Your Way to a $100 Million Investment Advisory Business

by RUSS ALAN PRINCE

KAREN MARU FILE

Best Wishes

Russ Alan Prince

Building Your Business—Marketing Your Way to a $100 Million Investment Advisory Business

by Russ Alan Prince and Karen Maru File

HNW Press

HNW Press
76 Penfield Road
Fairfield, CT 06430
Tel. 203-255-8772
Fax 203-256-9147

Printed in the United States of America. Printing number 1

Library of Congress Cataloging in Publication Data ISBN
ISBN number 0-9658391-0-9

Cover and book design by:
LUNA Corporate Design
Carina Krischlunas and Karin Johnson
50 Brinsmayd Avenue
Stratford, CT 06497
Tel. 203-378-2543

Other books by the authors: Russ Alan Prince and Karen Maru File

Published by Institutional Investor, tel. 212-224-3800
Cultivating the Affluent II: Leveraging High-Net-Worth Client and Advisor Relationships (©1997)
Cultivating the Affluent: How to Segment and Services the High-Net-Worth Market (©1995)

Published by National Underwriter, tel. 800-543-0874
Marketing to the Affluent: A Toolkit for Life Insurance Professionals (©1995)
Marketing to Family Business Owners: A Toolkit for Life Insurance Professionals (©1995)
Marketing through Advisors: A Toolkit for Life Insurance Professionals (©1996)
Building an Affluent Clientele: Marketing Personal Lines to the Wealthy (©1996)

Published by Jossey-Bass, tel. 888-378-2537
Seven Faces of Philanthropy (©1994)

Published by Lexington House, tel. 800-356-5936
Charitable Estate Planning Process: How to Find and Work with the Philanthropic Affluent (©1994)

Books written by: Russ Alan Prince

Published by National Underwriter, tel. 800-543-0874
The Charitable Giving Handbook (©1997)

Published by PMIC, tel. 800-633-7467
Physician Financial Planning in a Changing Environment (©1996)

In memory of Jerome Prince
- Russ Alan Prince

To Joe, Charlie and Mike
- Karen Maru File

To be involved in the on-going Building Your Business program, and recieve periodic informational supplements FREE, please fill out the following form and send it to:

HNW Press
76 Penfield Road
Fairfield, CT 06430

Or fax the completed form to: 203-256-9147

Yes, I would like to be involved in the on-going ***Building Your Business*** *program*

Name ____________________

Title ____________________

Name of Company ____________________

Address ____________________

____

Phone ____________________

Fax ____________________

Email ____________________

Table of Contents

Preface

We spend a good portion of our professional lives with elite producrs and highly motivated producers who want to "fast-track" to elite status. We have come to believe that tomorrow's elite producers will be those who chart new paths through the rapidly changing financial services environment. One path we already see is the opportunity to build a business by providing investment advisory services.

This path has its rewards, as some are already proving. But this path is not for everyone. Most of the elite producers we work with are not independent. They have become elite producers as stock brokers, as career insurance agents, as relationship managers inside private banks, as attorneys and as portfolio managers. In the future many producers will become elite, following the tried and true paths of their various specialties. And, there will be some who attain elite status by becoming independent investment advisors as well. Change in financial services is opening up new opportunities.

We also work with resource warehouses helping them become more responsive and therefore more successful to these industry changes. From strategic market planning to product and service development and positioning, we assist resource warehouses.

Our orientation however, is limited to the high-net-worth market. Our expertise on the purchasers of financial and related services is restricted to the affluent and to the small and mid-sized institutions they control (e.g., family offices, privately controlled firms, professional practices, endowments and foundations, etc.).

Recently, the elite producers and the resource warehouses we work with have been asking us to put to paper some of the ways an investment advisor can join the ranks of the elite producers. This idea took form as we saw the growth of the number of independent investment advisors and even larger growth in the assets they control. It made sense to us that a book on this corner of the producer world would make sense.

This book is written for several groups of people. We believe it will be useful to:

- Current independent investment advisors.
- The resource warehouses who support independent investment advisors. As products and services become commodities, the emphasis on value-added services will increase and take on a more strategic role.
- Elite producers who want to consider the independent investment advisory business to leverage their current client relationships.
- Producers in the growth stage of their career who aspire to be the best of the best. Some of these will want to go independent. We hope this book will help them make informed decisions.
- Producers interested in marketing financial services to the affluent and those interested in knowing more about affluent psychology.

With the restructuring of the financial industry, becoming an independent investment advisor is a career option that is here to stay. But it is important recognize that the mainstay of the financial industry — the brokerage firms, the insurance companies, the banks and investment management firms — are also here to stay. In our view, there will always be the large firms and the boutiques.

Currently, most producers are wondering if being independent is the right move for them. In some cases, it is. In many, many cases, it is not. We have seen top investment advisors go independent and succeed brilliantly, and we have seen some fail. Material in this book should help you decide if going independent is for you.

Finally, we pride ourselves on our track record of helping producers become dramatically more successful. Many of the processes and method we learned the hard way — in the field — are provided here. By using the tools and techniques in this book you, too, can build you business. With these guidelines, you can put significantly more assets under management. You, too can become an elite producer, one of the best of the best.

Russ Alan Prince
Karen Maru File
Connecticut
May, 1997

Forward

Having been in the insurance and financial planning business for over 15 years, I had established a very successful practice and a good lifestyle. I belonged to the Million Dollar Round Table. I have won all the awards from the companies I have worked with.

However, I felt I had reached a plateau in my career and wanted to go to the next level. It was clear to me that the next level was in fee-based money management and not in commission sales. The problem was that there was little useful information available to assist me in making the transition.

I began by logically thinking through the methodology of fee-based money management and what I needed to do to reach my goals. I knew I had to develop a marketing plan to get me to affluent investors. Like most high level insurance sales people I was very good at selling and very poor at marketing. It was not long before I realized I needed expert advice on developing a marketing strategy to begin to provide fee-based money management services for the wealthy.

I began working with Russ Prince of Prince & Associates over two years ago. I told Russ my goal was to get $100 million under fee-based management in five years. Russ looked at my operation and said I needed an overhaul. He felt that with my current structure it would be impossible to realize this goal without completely changing my marketing strategy and the way I do business. We started working together to facilitate these changes and learn the principles involved to accomplish my goals. Working with Russ, we developed a model for planners to make the transition from commission sales to fee-based money management that is both effective and efficient.

In a very short time I developed the expertise to identify and work with affluent investors. I have strong relationships with these wealthy investors, and have become their trusted advisor and their friend as well. I manage their pension plan assets as well as their discretionary funds. As we planned, my current client base has responded very favorably to this transition. Many have done more business with me than ever before.

After two years of applying the principles in this book, I now have a fee-based money management business that is efficient and focused. I learned to leverage relationships with my peers as well as the relationships with the companies I work with. I am not only on track for my goals, I am well ahead of schedule to attaining the $100 million under management.

I selfishly claim some of the credit for this book because I promoted the idea to put it together. I served as the first model for the philosophy and now have a model fee-based money management practice. The model is transferable if you commit to the principles and are disciplined about applying them. I have done it and I have made it work!

Building Your Business has all the information you will need to develop a $100 million fee-based money management practice. This book will help you better understand the financial services industry, and it will open your eyes to all the opportunities available.

If you wish to create a $100 million advisory practice, Building Your Business will give you the road map to follow. But you cannot simply read the book and put it on the shelf. You must commit to changing the way you do business and apply these principles on a daily basis. I am sure that if you do this in a very short time you will also become one of the best of the best.

Gary L. Rathbun, CLU, ChCF
Private Wealth Consultants, Savage and Associates, Inc.
Toledo, Ohio
May, 1997

1

The Right Market at the Right Time

1

Where the Money Is

"The thing that differentiates people from animals is money."
- Gertrude Stein

"Money alone sets the world in motion."
- Publilus Syrus

When he is asked what work he does, Russ likes to say "I study rich people." When people ask him why he studies rich people, he likes to tell the Willie Sutton story. Here is how it goes. Willie Sutton was once asked why he robbed banks. He answered, "'Cause that's where the money is." Russ studies rich people because the affluent market is where the money is.

In fact, the affluent market has been the most consistently profitable market for financial services, especially investment advisory services, for years. Not only has it been the most consistently profitable market, it is attractive right now for another reason. It is growing, and growing fast. At a time when other investment management markets are stagnating or even contracting, the number of wealthy individuals in search of investment advisory services is growing, and growing quickly.

Another reason the affluent market is "where the money is," is that affluent investors represent an annuity business. In no other market can you have the type of client loyalty you can have with the wealthy. Of course, this loyalty is not an automatic event, you must carefully nurture it. But once you have, through the magic of relationship management strategies, each and every one of your affluent clients will represent a consistent revenue stream for you.

Fortunately, for people who make their money in the affluent market, it is highly fragmented. The size of the financial institution[1] providing services to the affluent investor is not a determinant of success. In fact, big size is many times counter-productive. This means you can be an independent investment advisor, compete head-to-head with the largest financial firms, and you can come out a winner.

It's Profitable

We are often asked how profitable the independent investment advisory business can be. The answer has a number of parts. In the first place, there is no getting around the fact that the cost of getting new affluent investor clients is high. In our studies, we find that the first year of an independent advisory business is often "revenue-neutral,"[2] with profitability taking off in year two and sometimes not until year three. On the other hand, once your investment advisory business is established, the potential for increasing revenue per affluent investor, and the potential for leveraging each affluent investor relationship, is quite high. And, we have already mentioned that the annuity nature of the private wealth management business is one of its most attractive qualities.[3]

Another way to assess the profitability of the affluent private wealth market is to look at it in context. If we step back and look at the investment management business in general (as in Exhibit 1.1)[4], we can see that there are three strategically important categories of clients — retail clients, institutional clients, and affluent clients — and they are sensitive to cost and investment performance to different degrees.

We find, when we benchmark against the very best investment advisors, that they have a knack for managing the relationship with their affluent clients in such a way that their clients are actually relatively less cost-sensitive than either retail or institutional clients. We also find that they are able to manage client relationships in such a way that their affluent clients are also relatively less performance-sensitive. Retail clients, on the other hand, are known for their sensitivity to investment performance issues as well as their attention to cost issues. Affluent clients are more attractive than institutional clients, who tend to be highly sensitive to pricing considerations and moderately to highly sensitive to investment performance. Like you, thousands of investment advisors have looked at these choices and made their pick. After all, which type of client would you prefer to work with?

Exhibit 1.1 ATTRACTIVENESS OF THE AFFLUENT INVESTOR SEGMENT

Factors	Retail Investor	Institutional Investor	Affluent Investor
Price Sensitivity	★★	★★★	★
Performance	★★★	★★★	★

★★★ = High ★★ = Moderate ★ = Low

Source: Prince, R.A., McBride, W.J., & File, K.M. The Charitable Estate Planning Process: How to Find and Work with the Philanthropic Affluent. KY: Lexington House, 1994.

And, there is yet another reason to work with the affluent market. Simply put, the wealthy will always be with us. Through economic booms and economic busts, we see that there has always been a moneyed class. Although their numbers have ebbed and flowed with changes in the economy, throughout history there has always been and always will be an economic elite.

The outlook for wealth accumulation is good; the baby boomers are entering their peak earning years, the U.S. economy has become globally competitive and the spread of capitalism worldwide has created many more opportunities to become rich. And, as long as there have been wealthy people, there have been professional advisors, necessary to assist them in managing their financial affairs.[5]

Although these reasons to target affluent investors should be compelling, there are still other reasons to focus an investment advisory business on the affluent segment. One reason is the sheer size of the opportunity. There are a lot of wealthy people in the United States, the wealthy are getting wealthier, and the number of people considered wealthy is growing.[6]

Finally, opportunities abound because the affluent market is actually currently underpenetrated by professional money managers. According to one estimate, only a third to a half of the investable assets of the affluent are being professionally managed. And, just 10% of the wealth of the affluent market is in the hands of high-end brokers.[7]

We wouldn't predict that all of these assets will find their way to investment professionals, but we are comfortable in projecting that a significant portion will. Over the next few years, we forecast rapid expansion of the volume of money under independent investment management, and that is the reason for this book.

Just How Big Is the Affluent Market?

Of all the reasons to pursue the affluent market by independent investment advisors, the most compelling is the sheer size of the market. All over the globe, and all over the Unites States, private wealth is booming. Whether you look at the aggregate amount of assets or the aggregate number of wealthy people, the numbers are way up.

Just consider what is happening in terms of the world's supply of investable assets. There will be a jump of $4.6 trillion just from incremental household savings from the developing economies through the year 2000. From 1992 to 2002, the net financial accumulation is projected to increase by $12 trillion in 1992 dollars.[8]

Starting with the global perspective, one estimate puts the number of individuals with $1 million or more in investable assets at 3.3 million throughout the world. These 3.3 million affluent individuals are estimated to have a total of $7.6 trillion (USD) in investable assets.[9] Other estimates put the value of the U.S. market alone at $5 trillion[10], including the 2 million households with investable assets of $1 million. Yet a third estimate begins with a global market size of $9.6 trillion, and forecasts a year 2000 private wealth market of $17 trillion in assets if a 10% annual growth rate is assumed (see Exhibit 1.2).

We think the 10% growth rate figure may actually be on the low side, as the affluent portion of the population is growing in assets faster than it is growing in people. In the U.S., you are familiar with this phenomenon as the bifurcation of wealth, and the finding that the income and asset gap between rich and poor is increasing.[12] Our research shows that a 10% to 20% growth in assets is more

Exhibit 1.2 SIZING THE GLOBAL HIGH-NET WORTH MARKET

accurate, and this growth is resulting in a boom market for investment advisory services. While there are political issues rising due to the increasing division between rich and poor, the fact remains that there are many new affluent investors, that their numbers continue to grow, and that the assets they control are also growing. By the end of the century, there is projected to be an 80% increase in the number of households earning $100,000 or more per year.[13]

Taking any one of these estimates, the affluent market is large. It's even bigger when you consider that, in our judgment, most of these numbers are actually underestimates. There are several reasons for this. First, the wealthy seek to minimize their taxable income, and so will appear — statistically — less well off than they actually are. The other reason is that the source of wealth for many is a privately owned business, and private business ownership provides many opportunities to accumulate assets without them appearing as private wealth.[14] For these reasons, we believe that the affluent market is, if anything, significantly underestimated.[15]

What Are the Additional Investment Business Opportunities?

The scale and rate of growth of the affluent investor market is sufficient reason to target it for your investment advisory services. But you should also be aware of the many additional opportunities for growing your business by developing a clientele in this segment.

One of the most significant of these opportunities lies in opportunities for management of the assets of the businesses many of the affluent own. Many independent investment advisors we meet with are successfully targeting asset pools directly or indirectly controlled by their wealthy clients. They have found that through their personal and professional relationships, the affluent have significant influence over many investment management decisions. They often own companies, and the retirement plan assets of those companies represent attractive investment management opportunities.

Many high-net-worth individuals have established private foundations, the assets of which represent another opportunity. Still other affluent individuals have family offices in which they are key decision makers (see Appendix A). As a result, by targeting the affluent individual investment market, you are also positioned to capture significant institutional investment advisory business.

It Is Wide Open Territory

There is wide open territory in the private wealth industry at this time because it is extensively fragmented.[16] Many financial advisors are becoming independent because there are relatively low barriers to entry. The transition to independence can be brought about with a loyal affluent client following, a handle on back-office and product technology, and skills development in areas such as practice management and marketing. Of these factors, the relationship nature of the business translates into the potential for independent investment advisors like yourself to succeed no matter the extent of the institutional competition.

A Fragmented Industry

The investment management business focused on the affluent is highly fragmented. That is, no one player (i.e., financial institution or provider of services) has a dominant position. Consider the numbers: although there are 2 million liquid millionaires in the United States, no investment advisor appears to have more than 1% of the affluent market.[17]

Looking ahead, we do not expect this situation to change. We project that the market will stay fragmented. The reason for this is that there are few emerging technologies or economies of scale that benefit large institutions. On the other hand, there are decided benefits to being smaller. Smaller institutions, smaller investment advisory firms, can pay closer attention to clients. Investment management for the affluent is a relationship business. Even though much of the investment management business is driven by technology, it remains the interpersonal relationships between advisor and high-net-worth clients that prove to be the cornerstone to success. We find, over and over again, that it is "client-facing" activities that produce positive results.[18]

Investment management with the affluent is also a knowledge business. It revolves on "what" you know as well as "who" you know.[19] The "who" you know is critical to prospecting. For this reason, the independent investment advisor of the future will be very much like the traditional European private banker – a friend, a counselor, a financial advisor and an entrepreneur. Those who are capable of these roles will be highly successful. It is the individual advisor, not the financial institution, who has the edge in client referrals and higher "share of portfolio."

High Profit Potential Draws A Crowd

Of course, the profitability of the affluent investor market has not gone unnoticed. With competitive pressures ravaging their core businesses, institutional money management firms are looking to other markets. Too, the traditional money managers of pension funds are attracted to the affluent market because the fees they can earn are double what they earn on institutional accounts.[20]

Besides the pension money managers, the pension consultants are also moving down-market because they are increasingly finding the moneymaking prospects of their institutional clientele to be profit-neutral. This has motivated them to look for new types of clients. All of these new players — institutional money managers, pension fund money managers and pension consultants — are moving in to serve the needs of the individual high-net-worth investor.[21]

Another competitive element is retail institutions. Many providers of investment products to retail clients are moving up-market. For example, in a study of 138 family offices with

$100 million or more net worth, 17.2% were investing in mutual funds in 1996 and by 2001, 22.9% are expecting to invest in mutual funds.[22] Another example of the decision to move up-market are the mutual fund companies taking action to provide customized financial services to the affluent.

Advantage: The Independent Investment Advisor

It would be easy to become quite concerned about the number of institutional competitors for the affluent market. Certainly, all competition should be taken seriously. But the structural advantages currently favor independent investment advisors. At its core, this is a business of trust and strong interpersonal relationships. The financial advisor who has the trust and confidence of the affluent client will be successful over the long term in this business.

The reason for this is that the economic elite do not think of themselves as having relationships with financial institutions, although many financial institutions try to encourage this type of thinking. While affluent investors might walk into a name investment management firm, they just enter the firm in order to meet with an individual whom they trust. If that person were to leave, the odds are, his or her clients would follow.

It is very hard to take a personal advisor-client relationship and make it an institution-client relationship. We find very few instances where an advisor-client relationship has been successfully institutionalized. In those few instances where this is the case, the financial institution has created bonds with its affluent clients that supersede any personal bonds that develop with its people,[23] but these examples are rare.

Of course, the "name" of a financial institution can carry some weight in motivating a wealthy prospect to consider doing business with an individual within the firm. But when we talk with affluent clients, we find that the personal relationship is the number one factor in their selection of an investment advisor; the reputation of the firm that advisor is affiliated with is lower on their list of priorities. Affluent clients often explain that they "don't hire companies, we hire people." For most of the wealthy, a company or institutional name has nominal drawing and conversion power.

Yet another set of factors which confer a competitive advantage to the individual advisor are technological. Until recently, investment advisors had to affiliate with an institution to gain access to the technology necessary to provide the full range of investment advisory and related services to their affluent clients. With the breakthroughs and reshaping of technology, distributed processing and the structure of the industry itself, advisors can become independent of institutions. This trend is fundamentally restructuring the investment advisory industry. If an investment advisor and an affluent investor want to use a particular money manager, those services can be provided and the affluent client remains the client of the investment advisor. Advisors are now in the position of being able to outsource every single financial service and/or product. The result of technology is the effective elimination of all barriers to entry into serving the needs of the affluent, and capital requirements are also minimal.

The fact that this is a people business has a downside. You have to recognize that, from the perspective of the wealthy, this is not a business of financial institutions but of people. As a result, your competition includes all the other investment advisors, attorneys, accountants, brokers, insurance agents, bankers, investment managers, financial planners, and consultants who, like you, have been attracted to the profitability of the affluent market. And, there are many of these individuals.

To say there are many may be an understatement. There are over 400,000 brokers of National Association of Security Dealers member firms alone. There are more than 250,000 insurance agents, and about 10% of them are the extremely successful members of the Million Dollar Roundtable. There are more than 30,000 financial planners.

And there are the people who are still working with affluent clients from a position within an institution. There are 24,000 firms which are registered investment advisors. There are more than 50,000 private banks. These firms and banks employ many people. Add to these figures accountants, attorneys, and consultants, and you can see how competitive the affluent market has become. It is not at all surprising that there is such tremendous interest in the affluent market; it is rewarding.

Going Forward

- The opportunities that exist for investment advisors because of the number and wealth of affluent investors are considerable.

- Providing investment advisory services to the affluent is a profitable business.

- The market is attractive because it is fragmented, which creates many opportunities for independent investment advisors.

- The greatest loyalty bond exists between the individual advisor and the affluent client; affluent clients have comparatively low loyalty to institutions.

- Technological and structural changes have made it possible for more and more advisors to "go independent".

- In addition to personal money management services, there are additional business opportunities, of which the most significant are institutional money management services.

$

[1] Size is often measured by number of employees. This measure has never been shown to impact on the selection of a money manager. Further, assets under management is used in the selection process by only 12.9% of affluent investors. See: Prince, R.A., and File, K.M. Cultivating the Affluent: How to Segment and Service the High-Net-Worth Market. N.Y.: Institutional Investor, 1995.

[2] The assumption of a revenue-neutral first year is predicated on analyses from a wide range of financial institutions including independent investment advisors. What was quite informative is that until we were called in, these investment advisors were not computing this information. Additionally, the investment advisors rarely took into account total client value. It is usually worthwhile to develop a broad-stroke ability to ascertain the financial break points with respect to client acquisition and maintenance.

[3] Extensive surveys of financial institutions seeking to enter the investment advisory business for affluent individuals identify a number of factors contributing to this decision. Always among the top two or three is the annuity nature of the business. The same findings are found in surveys of financial advisors who are interested in expanding their practices in the investment advisory business.

[4] Prince, R.A., McBride, W.J., & File, K.M. The Charitable Estate Planning Process: How to Find and Work with the Philanthropic Affluent. KY: Lexington House, 1994.

[5] While there is a great deal of talk at private banking and money management conferences about technology replacing relationship managers and the increasing sophistication of affluent investors, we believe client facing behaviors will remain a critical component of this business for some time to come.

[6] Maude, D. & Molyneux, P. Private Banking: Maximizing Performance in a Competitive Market. London: Euromoney Publications, 1996.

[7] Goldstein, M.L. The Future of Money Management in America: 1997 Edition. N.Y.: Bernstein Research, 1997.

[8] Bryan, L. & Farrell, D. Market Unbound. NY: John Wiley & Sons, 1996.

[9] Bicker, L. Private Banking in Europe. London: Routledge, 1996.

[10] Goldstein, M.L. The Future of Money Management in America: 1997 Edition. N.Y.: Bernstein Research, 1997.

[11] ibid.

[12] For a discussion of the bifurcation "problem" see: Inhaber, H., and Carroll, S. How Rich is Too Rich? Income and Wealth in America. N.Y.: Praeger, ©1992. and Woldd, E.N. Top Heavy: A Study of the Increasing Inequality of Wealth in America. N.Y.: The Twentieth Century Fund Press, 1995.

[13] Linden, F. Consumer Affluence: The Next Wave. N.Y.: The Conference Board, 1994.

[14] Quite often it is exceedingly difficult to separate a business owner's private and corporate wealth. For a detailed analysis of the family business owner market see: Prince, R.A., and File, K.M., Marketing to Family Owned Businesses: A Toolkit for Life Insurance Professionals. OH: National Underwriter, 1996.

[15] The sizing of the affluent market is complicated further by extreme forms of illegal wealth such as drug dealing. For an excellent discussion of the shadow world of private wealth, albeit a somewhat dated one, see: Walter, I., Secret Money: The Shadow World of Tax Evasion, Capital Flight and Fraud. MA: Lexington Books, 1985. It is nevertheless important to recognize that this shadow world of private banking — broadly defined — constitutes, by all estimates, one of the largest flows of money (estimates are in the multiple trillions) which are also available for professional management.

[16] In contrast to the fragmentation that exists with respect to the affluent investor market, the institutional market is predicted to consolidate. There are too many money management companies chasing too few new pools of assets. See: Hurley, M.P., Meers, S.I., Bornstin, B.J. & Strumingher. The Coming Evolution of the Investment Management Industry: Opportunities and Strategies. N.Y.: Goldman Sachs, 1995.

[17] It is important to remember that almost all affluent investors retain more than one investment advisor. Thus, even if a player has thousands of clients, many of those affluent clients are also employing other advisors.

[18] Bicker, L. Private Banking in Europe. London: Routledge, ©1996.

[19] ibid.

[20] Coen, F.J. et al. Great Expectations: The Challenge of Serving the Super-Wealthy. Washington, D.C.: The Advisory Board Company, ©1996.

[21] Not only have many pension consultants taken steps to offer their consulting services to the affluent, they are also moving into money management. Both directly, and more often through independent investment advisors, pension consulting firms are taking steps to provide investment advisory services to the wealthy. Examining the pension consulting firms that are targeting the affluent, we find that the boutique firms have garnered the greatest success to date. These smaller firms bring technical expertise to the table and they tend to be hungrier, so they put in the time and effort to work with affluent investors just as independent investment advisors do.

[22] The research was conducted by Prince & Associates for Greystone Partners. The study examined the family financial strategies and world views of 138 family offices.

[23] To accomplish this requires a top-down relationship management process. The relationship managers in the firm are all acting pretty much the same. They will respond to affluent clients very similarly. Thus, they become interchangeable. Although a number of financial firms have attempted to establish such a system, there is a risk of it failing because relationship managers are not comfortable being so scripted. Interestingly, among the handful of firms that have made this approach work.

2

The Best of the Best

"Wine maketh merry: but money answereth all things."
Ecclesiastes 10:19

"Some people's money is merited,
And other people's is inherited."
Ogden Nash

A market as large and as profitable as the affluent market for investment advisory services should attract the "best of the best". And it does. As top investment and client relationship talent are beginning to break out, we are learning more and more about who some of the best of the best investment advisors are, and what makes them so successful.

Before we go on. Of course there are many, many excellent investment advisors who choose not to break out, not to leave the financial institutions they're working in. And there are some indifferent performers who are giving life as an independent investment advisor a try. But we are going to use the term "best of the best" to refer to the top independent investment advisors because our research has shown that, as a group, they engender higher levels of client satisfaction, instill more loyalty, and are more entrepreneurial.

A Checklist

When it comes to getting and keeping affluent investors as clients, independent investment advisors are, without question, some of the very best financial advisors there are. Empirical comparisons with other types[1] of financial advisors show that this is so. Moreover, independent investment advisors are recognized by other types of financial advisors as significant competitive threats, as we'll discuss in Chapter 3.

Why are independent investment advisors some of the best of the best? There are a lot of answers to this one, but we like to reach into evolutionary biology for some insight into structural causes. The sociological tenets of Darwinian determinism[2] are useful here in helping us predict not only who will survive, but who will thrive. According to Darwinian determinism, when there is a change in the environment, organisms which are able to adapt to the new conditions are more likely to thrive. Organisms which cannot adapt not only do not thrive, their very survival may be threatened. This insight from evolutionary biology has been used to explain sociological phenomenon like the urban life and the corporation. It also offers us a metaphor for the financial services industry.

There have been massive changes in the financial services environment, principally technological. Some individuals have adapted very quickly to these changes; they have become independent investment advisors. Most of the independent investment advisors are thriving because they have realigned the way they function to the changes permeating the environment. Individuals like these, who are able to sense environmental changes, and who then capitalize on those changes, achieve a greater degree of success, and are referred to as the best of the best.[3]

It comes as no surprise, then, that the very challenges of the independent investment advisory market attract the successful, the producers with a proven track record, the advisors secure in the loyalty of their affluent client base. The ones who have been most successful working with all the support and resources an institution can provide are the ones ones who are most confident of their success when they have to create their own support systems. Investment advisors who need or value the support of institutions are most likely to stay working within them.

Since profound changes in the financial services industry make it increasingly easy to go independent, many of the very best financial advisors are choosing to be independent. At this stage of market evolution, high-end investment advisors share, to varying degrees, the following characteristics:[4]

Entrepreneurial

The best of the best are entrepreneurial. They are consummate business people with an instinct for the financial services business. They are dedicated students of the investment advisory field, and they have learned the ropes from years of "living in the trenches".

Like other entrepreneurs, independent registered investment advisors prefer to work in small organizations which they lead. Independent investment advisory firms tend to be small. Our recent research has shown that the average independent investment advisory firm has six people (with a range of two to twenty-five people).[5]

Although the firms are generally small, their impact is large. Independent investment advisory firms constitute a significant force in the financial services industry. These small firms have assets under management ranging from a few million to significantly over $200 million.[6] In this sector of the industry, the number of employees in the firm and the size of the asset base managed by the firm are not highly correlated.

These entrepreneurial firms are focused on growth. Independent investment advisors project they will double the assets they have under management over the next five years. About 15% forecast they will be managing $200 million or more.[7]

Technically Savvy

The best of the best have usually come into the field of independent investment advisor services from a wide variety of backgrounds. Some were investment advisors or brokers who used to work for wirehouses. Some were insurance agents who have left the career agency system. Some were accountants or attorneys who have shifted the emphasis of their private practices.

What the best of the best share is technical sophistication. Regardless of which route they took into the field, the best of the best are not afraid of learning technical aspects of other products and services they need to create a stronger position with their affluent clientele. That's why we see insurance agents who have expanded their practice to selling comprehensive investment services. That's why many brokers and investment advisors now are adept at estate and tax planning. That's why attorneys and accountants have expanded into financial planning from their core competencies. The best of the best understand the complex and integrated needs of the affluent and are determined to provide them.

Take estate planning. Most of the best of the best can already offer high level and comprehensive estate planning services for their affluent clients.[8] Estate planning is a natural extension of investment planning, given the age of many of the affluent. Estate planning makes strategic sense as well when you consider the many trillions of dollars that will be moving from one generation to another over the next decade or two.[9] Estate planning also makes sense from a relationship management perspective, as it enables you to learn about all the assets of the affluent investor.[10] The typical affluent investor retains several advisors, spreading their investable assets among them. The best of the best know this, and work to find ways to get an overview of the entire asset position, and implement asset capture strategies to bring more under their management.[11] The best of the best use the fact-finding process of estate planning to set the stage to motivate the affluent investor to switch assets from other investment advisors to them.[12]

The best of the best have also become involved in the technical aspects of charitable giving.[13] They recognize that many affluent investors are attracted to charitable estate planning. Charitable estate planning is the process of redistributing assets to maximize their value while enabling the philanthropic affluent to be charitable in ways that work best for them.[14] Charitable estate planning therefore not only results in the creation of charitable gifts, it also has all the benefits for the independent investment advisor of estate planning. Like estate planning (of which is it a part) charitable estate planning is an effective way of gathering data on the total asset profile of the affluent investor. The best of the best have mastered the technical aspects of the charitable remainder trust, recognizing in it a versatile financial planning tool that is an effective and profitable environment for managing assets. On average, charitable remainder trusts result in 25 years of money management fees.

Not all financial advisors are very technically knowledgeable. Some remain unskilled in the use of estate planning instruments such as private foundations, the charitable remainder trust,[15] or in the benefits these may have for affluent investors.[16] However, those investment advisors who master the technical aspects of these strategies will be able to compete alongside the best of the best, to compete effectively against the largest financial institutions.

The same arguments apply to asset protection planning.[17] Many affluent investors are concerned about the potential of financially costly lawsuits. This is not an unfounded concern; in a recent period, one out of five physicians was the target of litigation[18]. As with charitable estate planning, there is a tremendous overlap between asset protection planning and estate planning.[19] Thus, by providing asset protection planning services, the best of the best are able to obtain similar benefits. They often find that asset protection planning is easier to position to the affluent; many wealthy individuals are not interested in estate planning but are very interested in asset protection planning.[20]

Sensitive to People

Whether it's managing their firms or working with affluent investors, the best of the best are able to develop levels of rapport that inspire trust as well as heart-felt respect and commitments from others.

The best of the best have developed patterns of loyalty among their clientele, and when they are ready, they lead their clients out of their previous firm and into their own practice. When the best of the best leave their previous affiliations and go independent, they bring with them the overwhelming majority of their affluent clientele.[21] As a result, their new business starts with a critical mass of clients already on board, and a revenue stream is already created.

Bottom Line Oriented

Independent investment advisors are predominantly compensated in any one, or a combination, of three ways:

To maximize short term revenue you are advised to adopt all three compensation approaches. However, your ability to work in a fee-based environment will result in the long term viability of your practice with the affluent.[22]

Exhibit 2.1 MAJOR FORMS OF COMPENSATION

Asset-based management fees	**You get a fee, calculated as a percentage of assets undermanagement, for the length of time the assets remain with you. The industry convention is 1% of the value of the portfolio where the fee decreases as the size of the portfolio increases.**
Fees for financial advice and planning	**You charge fees, by the project or by the hour, for your expertise. For example, if you were to design an estate plan for an affluent client, you might charge $3,000.**
Commissions	**You receive a payment when you sell a product. For example, front-loaded and back-end loaded shares of mutual funds pay commissions.**

Increased competition for affluent investors is slowly educating them to the way financial professionals are compensated. Their preferred method of paying for your expertise is asset-based management fees and fees for financial advice and service.[23]

Aside from affluent investor preference, two additional reasons are propelling the popularity of fee-based compensation.[24] One, it puts you on the same side as the affluent investor. Your revenues are tied, to a large degree, to the value of your advice. This is quite appealing to the wealthy investor. Two, it enables you to be compensated for not taking action when this is the right course of action.

Today, few investment advisors are purely fee-based (or fee-only) advisors. Most investment advisors still generate commission revenues from the sale of financial products such as life insurance or annuities. Still, the trend is toward the fee-based system, particularly for investment products. Because of this trend, the number of fee-only independent investment advisors is expected to increase five-fold over the next five years.[25]

Global

The best of the best are emerging around the world. The trend toward independent investment advisors is not limited to the United States. In Chapters 7 and 9 we find that throughout the world financial advisors are carefully evaluating the risks and rewards of going independent. The prevalence of independent investment advisors varies around the world. In Central and South America, the trend toward independent investment advisors is just beginning to take off. In Canada and in Europe, the trend toward independence is entering its growth phase.[26] In the Pacific Rim, the market is more mature; independent investment advisors have always had an established position.

A Leading Indicator

An extremely effective way to understand one industry is to look at another one that is structurally similar and draw informative parallels. In examining the structural dynamics constituting the world of independent investment advisors, we find quite a number of industries from which we can learn. There is the franchise industry, as well as the management consulting business.

In fact, any industry where the distribution system is independent of manufacturing resembles, in some ways, the world of independent investment advisors. However, the closest and most meaningful comparison exists between independent investment advisors and high-end insurance agents.

The World of High-End Insurance Agents

The way in which the independent investment advisor industry is evolving very closely parallels many of the transitions that have worked their way through the insurance industry. In stage one of market development, most producers were closely affiliated with one primary insurance company, and received most of their compensation for selling the products of that company to their clients. In stage two, the high-end agents found they needed access to a wider diversity of products to serve the needs of their affluent clients, and they began to widen their institutional affiliations. This move, however, weakened them from the point of view of negotiating favorable arrangements with institutions and customizing product, because they brought less business to any given institution. Before long, in stage three, these independent, high-performing producers joined together in producer networks to obtain better terms from institutions. As you can see, the high-end independent investment advisor is a first cousin to the high-end insurance agent.[27]

This three stage market evolution provides interesting insights for independent investment advisors and the financial institutions they work with. By learning the lessons elite insurance agents had to learn the hard way, independent investment advisors and financial firms which seek to provide them with services will be able to develop more productive working relationships much more quickly. The growth of advisor networks among independent investment advisors, for instance, parallels the stage three development of insurance agent producer and study groups.

Exhibit 2.2 THREE STAGES OF MARKET EVOLUTION

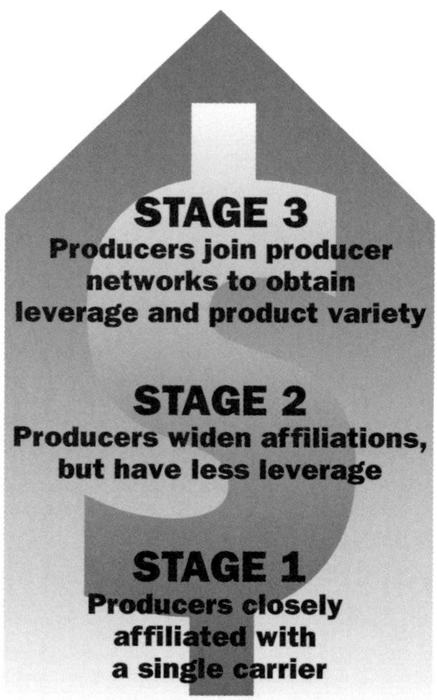

Because of the structural similarities between high-end insurance agents and high-end independent investment advisors, we will draw on our work in understanding the "best practices" of elite insurance agents.[28]

Going Forward

- The best of the best are among the first to notice change in their environment, to adapt to change and to leverage the opportunities inherent in change.

- When it comes to independent investment advisory services, we can come up with a check list of what characterizes the best of the best:

  - Entrepreneurial.

  - Technically savvy.

  - Sensitive to people.

  - Bottom-line oriented.

  - Global.

- The evolution of the best of the best investment advisors parallels the recent evolution of high-end insurance producers, whose industry has just undergone a similar structural evolution. Their experience leads us to predict:

  - The growing power of independent advisors.

  - Their increasing control of the affluent market.

  - The development of producer groups to leverage their power vis-a-vis the institutions.

$

[1] By types of financial advisors we are considering broad categories such as broker, family office and so forth. Within each "type" there are exceptionally talented professionals who would succeed in most any environment. Nevertheless, for our purposes, we will look at the "types" thereby including these elite advisors with all that are striving to reach these heights.

[2] Darwinian determinism is predicated on the concept of survival of the fittest applied to specific genuses of social structural environments. The financial services industry respective to the affluent market due in large part to the fragmentation of this market is a classic case of the kind of environment in which Darwinian determinism would operate.

[3] As we noted, not all of the best of the best investment advisors choose to "go independent." We have extensive data which shows a large number of elite financial advisors find significant value working in supportive financial institutions. For instance, a number of these top investment advisors do not want to be involved with running a business, preferring instead to concentrate on client matters.

[4] Prince, R.A. "Insurance Agents Dominate the Upscale Markets." Probe, in press.

[5] These conclusions are based on the findings from the 1997 Survey of Independent RIAs part of the Strategic Market Insights Series conducted by Prince & Associates. In this study 461 independent registered investment advisors were surveyed to ascertain a strategic profile of the independent investment advisor, the sources they use to obtain mutual funds, their mutual fund selection behavior, the steps resource warehouses need to take to build strategic relationships with independent investment advisors, and the future products and services these advisors will offer the affluent. Some of the findings and conclusions from this research will be presented in this book.

[6] ibid.

[7] ibid.

[8] ibid.

[9] Many financial institutions are aggressively moving into the field of estate planning because of client demand for the services. For example, brokerage firms and large investment management firms, including mutual fund companies, have established trust companies and set up units

to do estate planning. On the basis of existing research it's clear that many of these firms are not being very effective. There are quite a number of reasons for their poor performance. One that stands out is due to the difference between marketing investment advisory services and marketing estate planning services. The latter is less product driven, more intricate (especially as you deal with wealthier and wealthier clients) and the sales cycle is materially different. Nevertheless, once these financial institutions recognize and appropriately respond to these differences, many will be very successful.

[10] While the estate planning process, when adroitly managed, will enable the advisor to gather investable assets, anecdotal evidence shows this is rarely done. On the other hand, when estate planning is done with an eye to the investable assets, the advisors are able to pick up a substantial portion of the wealthy investors' assets for management. High-end insurance agents have been remarkably successful in this regard.

[11] Prince R.A. & File K.M., Cultivating the Affluent: How to Segment and Service the High-Net-Worth Market. N.Y.: Institutional Investor, 1995.

[12] ibid. You will need to understand the motivations that lead to affluent investors switching money managers. Relationship considerations, for example, prove to be much more important than investment performance.

[13] 1997 Survey of Independent RIAs; Prince, R.A. "Affluent Seek Information on Giving." National Underwriter. 98 (39) 1994.

[14] Prince, R.A., McBride, W.J., & File, K.M. The Charitable Estate Planning Process: How to Find and Work with the Philanthropic Affluent. KY: Lexington House, 1994.

[15] Prince, R.A., Rathbun, G.L., & Steiner, C.E. The Charitable Giving Handbook. OH: National Underwriter, 1997.

[16] ibid.

[17] 1997 Survey of Independent RIAs

[18] Prince, R.A., Phillips, E. K., & Apolinsky, H.I. Physician Financial Planning in a Changing Environment. CA: PMIC, 1996.

[19] ibid.

[20] The flip-side of asset protection planning is settlement management. Investment advisors who work in this area regularly are instrumental in helping people manage significant sums.

[21] 1997 Survey of Independent RIAs.

[22] One variant that has some appeal is commission off-set. Here the affluent client pays you a fee for your financial advice and planning. You also sell products which pays you a commission. The commissions are used to lower, and even eliminate, the fees you've charged.

[23] Preliminary empirical research supported by extensive anecdotal reports clearly show that affluent investors are generally opposed to paying commissions for discretionary money management services. While many will pay loads because they want a particular fund, they are less inclined to pay investment advisors commissions. This is recognized by independent investment advisors as they intend to move away from load funds to no-load funds. See: 1997 Survey of Independent RIAs

[24] Murry, N. The Excellent Investment Advisor. NY: Nicholas Murry, 1996.

[25] 1997 Survey of Independent RIAs

[26] The very same reasons that are so clearly seen in among financial advisors in the United States is also in evidence throughout the world. The noted differences are the importance of the various reasons.

[27] We are discounting the fact that many high-end insurance agents are independent investment advisors and that about 60% of insurance agents want to be fee-based investment advisors.

[28] These "best practices" were derived by numerous extensive empirical studies enhanced by in-depth qualitative field work in the insurance industry. This multi-year program of research concentrates on the organizational structures of the industry that result in the highest degree of insurance agent productivity. Concurrently, the research deals with the psychology and the behavioral patterns of the most effective insurance agents — the multi-million dollar producers and those that do even better. Specifically, the most effective and productive insurance agents, the elite, are "life long learners." That is, they actively seek out new information that can be employed to enable them to improve their insurance practices. Part of this process entails working directly with financial institutions (i.e., insurance and other types of financial services companies) and their representatives (e.g., general agents and wholesalers) in a manner that

results in the financial institutions being the facilitators of desired information. Another part of this process entails the way they work together to become more capable. Finally, there are the ways they leverage expertise outside these circles to enhance their practices. It is these activities and systems that can be readily applied to the world of the independent investment advisor.

3

The Players

***"Money can beget money,
and its offspring can beget more, and so on."
- Benjamin Franklin***

***"To turn $100 into $110 is work.
To turn $100 million into $110 million is inevitable."
- Edgar Bronfman***

A market as attractive as the affluent investor market will attract some competitive players. When a market is attractive and also fragmented, it will attract even more players. When a market is attractive, fragmented and also undergoing deregulation and restructuring, it will attract a significant amount of competition. When there is intense competition, it is important to assess the relative strengths and weaknesses of the competition — the other players — compared to your own and those of the best of the best independent investment advisors.

The Lineup

The competitors for the investment business of the affluent ranges from private banks to family offices to independent investment advisors. All are seeking to carve out a position in the affluent investor market for themselves (see Exhibit 3.1).

Private Banks

For many years, private banks were the only significant players in the affluent market. Their market position has eroded due to competition and fragmentation, but private banks are seeking to re-establish their position as service integrators.[1]

Exhibit 3.1 COMPETITORS IN THE AFFLUENT INVESTOR MARKET

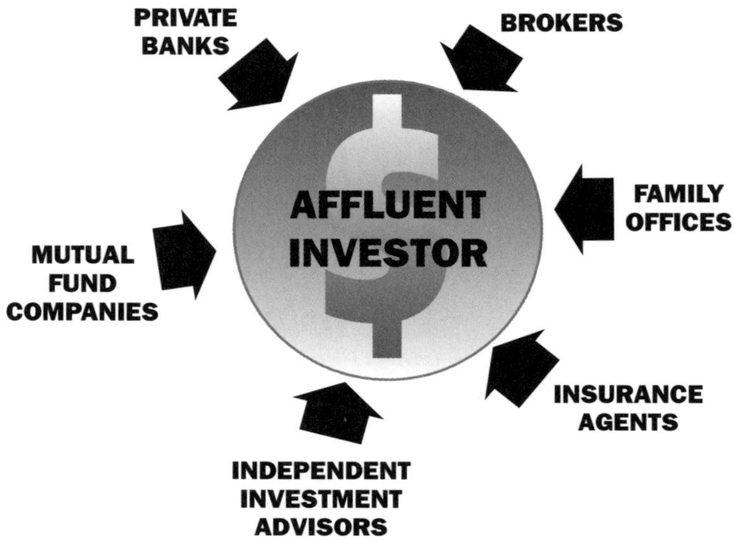

Since its inception, private banking has been the ultimate in client centered businesses.[2] One way to think about private banking is that it is any service the affluent client wants it to be. Private banks provide everything from wealth enhancement to wealth preservation to walking the dog in a pinch and checking on the house while clients are away.

The core business of private banks is money management services.[3] Trust and estate planning services are also typical.[4] It used to be that private banks had the trust area to themselves; now many other types of providers (from brokerage firms to mutual fund companies) are looking to compete in this arena.[5] Lending to the wealthy, an area once the sole preserve of private banks, is now a service offered by some other competitors.[6]

Private banks continue to serve the affluent market, but their share is much smaller than it once was. Across the board, other competitors have taken portions of the affluent market away.

Brokers

From the wirehouses to the regional and smaller brokerage firms, the affluent have often turned to brokers for investment advice. The broker's traditional business has been selling securities. However, the commission-based structure that was the cornerstone of the broker's offering is giving way to a fee-based approach, and the narrow focus on securities is being replaced by a wider one of investment management and financial planning.

Several factors foster this change. One is modern portfolio theory. There has been an evolution from the active trading of securities in order to realize gains to the buy and hold philosophy of diversification and asset allocation. This shift has created the need for a new approach to compensation. In addition, no-load mutual fund programs being adopted by brokerage firms, as well as the emphasis on Wrap programs, also drive the rethinking of the compensation structure. So, too, do the evolving preferences of affluent investors.

With a shift to fee-based compensation systems, the brokerage firms have initiated many programs to target the affluent market because it generates higher fee income. It is important to keep in mind that the average brokerage investor client is well below the affluent investor threshold. The typical broker does not have many affluent investors with $1 million or more in a discretionary investment account, Wrap account, or similar product. Actually, the average broker will have just 5% to 15% of his or her clients at this level.[7] The majority of clients will have fewer assets to invest.

Some brokerage firms are taking the initiative to create specialty groups to assist their brokers in finding and working with the affluent. Such groups bring a highly sophisticated approach to money management including more intricate products such as hedge funds and private equity deals. The brokerage firms are also taking steps to bring comprehensive financial planning to the affluent. These initiatives will enable brokers to meet a wide variety of the financial needs and wants of the affluent.[8]

Family Offices

In one sense, family offices are not new as wealthy families have been managing their own wealth, often with the assistance of a few advisors, for centuries. What is new is the recent rapid increase in the number of family offices. There are between 2,500 and 3,000 of them in the United States today,[9] and the concept is taking hold around the world among the most affluent.

Once enough assets have been accumulated, it makes more sense to hire investment advisors as employees rather than pay them fees and commissions. Once this happens, a family office is created. Roughly speaking, a minimum of about $50 million in investable assets should be available for a family office to prove-in economically, because of its high cost structure.[10] Traditionally, family offices have been established by members of a single family. A new trend is for families to pool assets in order to create a family office, or to offset family office costs by taking in other assets to be managed for a fee.

As a result, increasing numbers of family offices are direct competitors to investment advisors. While most family offices are on the look out for families with similar asset profiles, more and more are taking on the average liquid millionaire as a client. Quite a number of these family offices are actively engaged in portfolio management, although some retain investment advisors to provide selected investment services (see Appendix A).

Mutual Fund Companies

Mutual fund companies are a relatively late entrant. They have traditionally served independent investors, the people who like making their own decisions. But many of their investors have become affluent over the years, and now require more specialized advice. As a result, more and more mutual fund companies are creating dedicated units to address the particular needs of the high-net-worth investor. Mutual funds are gearing up to provide financial and investment planning, retirement and estate planning, charitable planning, insurance planning and tax planning.

Because of their scale and their customary way of doing business, most mutual fund companies will deliver these services with a mass market approach.[11] They will leverage technology rather than interpersonal relationships between advisor and client. Since the affluent are more responsive to one-on-one relationships, it may be unlikely that the mutual fund companies will attract more than a small segment of the affluent market unless they make significant investments in personnel. Still, a fair number of mutual fund companies will try, and some will succeed among the affluent clients less oriented to personal relationships. Keep in mind that not all mutual fund companies will establish private client groups.[12]

Insurance Agents

There is a strong push by the insurance industry to enable agents to be fee-based advisors. It's important to note that it is not the insurance companies that are driving the trend among insurance agents to become fee-based investment advisors. The insurance industry is responding to market demand and competitive pressures. The majority of insurance agents want to be in the investment advisory business, and many have taken steps to expand their business already. This has been relatively easy for insurance agents, as investment advice is a complementary service to what they currently provide.

Because of the limitations imposed by quite a few of the insurance company broker/dealers coupled with the structure of the insurance industry, a large percentage of these insurance agents will likely go independent. There is already a precedent; for high-end insurance agents to be independent or quasi-independent is often the norm.

The more insurance agents move to independent status, the more they shift to fee-based compensation, and the more they offer investment services, the more they will resemble brokers who have become independent investment advisors. Like brokers, there will be a number of top-producing insurance agents who will excel as investment advisors.

Anecdotal evidence shows us that the elite insurance agents are exceptional asset gatherers, possessing the marketing expertise and, more importantly, the contacts among the wealthy, to build $100 million investment advisory businesses relatively quickly. Interestingly, while we are identifying these investment advisors as insurance agents, because that is where they received their training, most of them are now independent investment advisors as well as very erudite financial advisors.

Independent Investment Advisors

There is a very powerful trend toward independence among financial advisors in the private wealth management industry. Brokers are evaluating the advantages and disadvantages of working for a brokerage firm. Insurance agents are considering the logic of providing investment advisory services under the umbrella of an insurance company. Relationship managers throughout the world, working in large investment firms as well as banks, are thinking about the benefits of going out on their own. And, portfolio managers are also considering their options, with independence being seriously considered.

Accountants who enter this field will do so as independent investment advisors. And we cannot forget all those who currently are independent investment advisors.

Certainly, in the short term, independent investment advisors are not going to dominate the private wealth industry and they never will. However, as we saw in the previous chapter, they are becoming more pronounced participants. Independent investment advisors are growing in number and in the proportional amount of assets they control. Taken together with the considerable interest so many financial advisors have in being independent, there is no doubt that, in the aggregate, independent investment advisors will prove to be a very powerful force. This perception is evidenced by the fact that so many in the private wealth industry are quite concerned about the "threat" posed by independent investment advisors.

The #1 Competitive Threat

While any individual financial advisor can be good or bad, successful or unsuccessful, from the perspective of competition, which type of financial advisor is the one other types of financial advisors are most concerned about? Who is the number ONE competitive threat? In other words, who worries whom?

To answer this question, a total of 1,687 financial advisors in the United States and Canada were surveyed in order to ascertain who they believed are their most worrisome competitors for affluent investors. Within the private banks, family offices and mutual fund companies, senior officers responsible for strategic planning or marketing were questioned. On the other hand, individual brokers, insurance agents and independent investment advisors were surveyed. Each of the advisors were asked to rate the extent to which their competitors — the other types of financial advisors — posed a significant threat to them and their efforts to cultivate affluent investors as clients. The overall results are shown in Exhibit 3.2.

Far and away, everyone agrees that the number ONE competitive threat is perceived to come from independent investment advisors. Nearly three in four competitors (73.4%) report that independent investment advisors pose a significant threat to them where the affluent investor is concerned. The reasons why we need only remind you. Independent investment advisors are likely to be the best of the best, moving rapidly with market changes, adapting their strategies effectively and quickly capitalizing on opportunities. Independent investment advisors are entrepreneurial, technically savvy, people oriented, and accustomed to leadership. Independent investment advisors are formidable competition for the loyalties of the affluent investor market.

Brokers are the next category of financial advisors most of the competitors (57.2%) are concerned with. Then come the mutual fund companies which 38.0% of their competitors are "worried about."

Less that one in five of the various financial advisors (17.4%) see private banks as a significant threat. Fewer competitors (8.9%) identify family offices as a threat. Part of the reason for this is the definition of affluent. Family offices are seen as usually targeting greater wealth. Competitors going after the "common millionaire" do not see themselves in competition with family offices for affluent investors.

Insurance agents are considered a threat by very few competitors (7.5%). Although insurance agents are taking steps to work in the private wealth management field (as we discussed in Chapter 2 and will return to in Chapter 6), at the present time they are not recognized as a competitor to be particularly concerned about.

Exhibit 3.2 PERCENTAGE OF WHO BELIEVE EACH TYPE OF ADVISOR IS A SIGNIFICANT COMPETITIVE THREAT

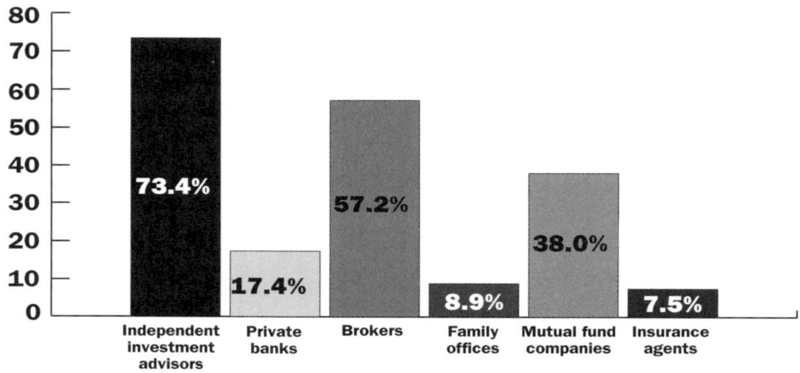

Based on information from 1,687 Financial Advisors

Competitor Perceptions by Competitor

By now, you may be saying, "I don't just want to know how competitors are viewed overall. I'm a broker and I want to see how other brokers assess the competition." This data is shown in Exhibit 3.3. Read across the rows to see how groups of respondents rated the threat of each competitor. For example, private banks are most concerned about independent investment advisors (69.3%), and mutual fund companies (55.6%). Brokers, mutual fund companies and insurance agents are clear that independent investment advisors are the single greatest competitive threat they face (94.9%, 87.1% and 93.4% respectively).

Exhibit 3.3 COMPETITOR PERCEPTIONS BY COMPETITOR

	Private Banks	Brokers	Family Offices	Mutual Fund Companies	Insurance Agents	Independent Investment Advisors
Private Banks		58.6%	25.7%	55.6%	8.3%	69.3%
Brokers	18.1%		6.0%	49.7%	18.3%	94.9%
Family Offices	21.5%	16.0%		11.8%	0.0%	22.2%
Mutual Fund Companies	14.5%	61.3%	3.2%		0.0%	87.1%
Insurance Agents	19.9%	79.3%	2.3%	44.1%		93.4%
Independent Investment Advisors	13.2%	70.7%	7.2%	28.7%	10.8%	

Based upon a survey of 1,687 financial advisors

When we look at the lineup of advisors seeking to build businesses in managing the assets of the affluent market, we can assess their relative strengths and weaknesses (see Exhibit 3.4). At a time when there is major structural change in market environments, the competitive advantage goes to those who are entrepreneurial, technically savvy and empathic. Our review of the key players in this market shows that only independent investment advisors are high on all three critical characteristics. Overall, independent investment advisors are the best of the best in terms of an entrepreneurial attitude, being technically knowledgeable and able to create great client loyalty. By comparison, other competitors rate less highly on these factors. Private banks, for example, are high when it comes to the special touches that make clients fiercely loyal, but don't follow through with technical proficiencies or innovative new products and services.

Exhibit 3.4 RATING THE CHARACTERS OF COMPETITORS

Competitors	Entreprenurial	Technically Saavy	People Focused
Independent Investment Advisors	★★★	★★★	★★★
Private Banks	★	★	★★★
Brokers	★★	★★	★★
Family Offices	★	★★★	★★
Mutual Funds Companies	★★	★★★	★★
Insurance Agents	★★★	★★	★★★

★★★ = High ★★ = Moderate ★ = Low

Going Forward

- The affluent market is so attractive it has always drawn significant competition. Traditional players include:
  - Private banks, long known for their emphasis on client service, which are trying to reposition themselves as a response to losing share.

- Brokerage firms, which are shifting to fee-based compensation systems and setting up affluent investor programs.

- Family offices, once the province of the most wealthy, are increasingly serving other wealthy families.

- Mutual fund companies have created a new generation of independent investors, and are now developing ways their core competency of mass marketing can be used to deliver augmented financial services to the affluent.

- Insurance agents have long recognized the appeal of the affluent market, and many are re-positioning themselves as investment advisors.

• However, it is the newest competitor, the independent investment advisor, who is widely perceived to be the number ONE competitive threat.

$

[1] The renaissance in private banking is based in part on the increasing strength of universal banks. However, for all the reasons the wealthy are such an attractive market, private banks (including trust companies) are finding themselves doing increasingly well. Strategically, the private banking business not only depresses earnings fluctuations, but when properly executed it generates significant new business for other areas of the bank such as corporate finance, transaction services and so forth.

[2] Bicker, L. Private Banking in Europe. London: Routledge, 1996.

[3] In a study of the business lines of private banks, asset management was identified as the primary offering. For the majority of private banks, all other services are intended to be feeders to asset management. This includes trust services.

[4] For our purposes, private banks encompass the complete array of services and products banks provide to the affluent. Operationally, many private banks are very product driven and usually that product is lending. Investment management and trusts services are offered out of the trust department.

[5] Most of the wirehouses, quite a number of regional brokerages, numerous mutual fund companies and a plethora of insurance companies all have their own trust companies. For the most part, many of these trust companies have yet to hit their numbers. The consultant-derived projections usually failed to take into account the utilization behaviors of the distribution systems. See: Prince, R.A., "If You Build It, Someone Might Even Show Up." Probe, in press.

[6] While numerous other financial institutions such as brokerage firms and insurance companies are creating the structures to provide credit to the affluent, banks will be the dominant provider in this field for quite some time.

[7] This estimate is based on an analysis of the top producers of two wirehouses and six regional brokerage firms. It does not include institutional investment advisory business conducted by these brokers, and nearly all those evaluated were engaged in such activities.

[8] A major problem with this approach is the ability to appropriately direct resources. To make such a system viable necessitates advanced training emphasizing the prospect identification function. Subsequently, a well developed screening system needs to be put in place. Finally, the internal structural arrangements bringing the required levels of expertise at the appropriate times, instead of whenever, must be set up. The evidence so far indicates that these efforts have not been undertaken. Instead, a much

more random approach has been pursued. The results have consequently been less than spectacular.

[9] This estimate is based on a Delphi analysis of 14 financial institutions and consultants who specialize in the family office market. We have a list of approximately 2,100 family offices. However, these tend to be the more visible firms. If you look outside the United States, the number of family offices is hypothesized to be in excess of 10,000. Some of them have been quite well established for years, and a greater number of them are relatively new.

[10] The $50 million criteria is a generally accepted one. The reason for this asset level is that a family office is not an inexpensive proposition. The returns and economies of scale that can be achieved with an investment pool of $50 million is generally sufficient to make the idea of a family office viable. Still, there are a number of families that have created family offices with a much lower initial asset pool. Additionally, there are many families considering the establishment of a family office who fail to meet this asset level. With the advances in technology, the ability of smaller family fortunes to become family offices is becoming a worthwhile endeavor.

[11] Preliminary analyses of mutual fund companies seeking to provide private client services find that there are a number of factors which are more inclined to result in success. One key factor is a recognition of the significant differences between affluent investors and retail investors. The mutual fund companies that are having minimal, if any success, are those that are simply trying to move upscale while still employing their retail marketing strategies and delivery systems. At the same time, the strategy of trying to duplicate the classic private bank look and feel will prove to be of limited, if any value, for most mutual fund companies. Instead, those mutual fund companies that will be quite successful in this endeavor will create a differentiated brand identity from other types of competitors, as well as proactively leveraging their retail operation while selectively marketing to new prospective affluent investor clients.

[12] Out of 61 randomly selected mutual fund companies who currently do not have dedicated affluent client units, 27.9% of them are in the process of creating such units. For many of these companies, what is slowing down the process from drawing board to the trenches is a combination of internal politics and some confusion over the critical success factors.

2

The Independent Investment Advisor Paradigm

4

The New Paradigm

"It is today possible, to a greater extent than at any time in the world's history, for a company to locate anywhere, to use resources from anywhere, to produce a product that can be sold anywhere."
- Milton Friedman

"The big opportunity for the rest of the decade is around companies transforming the way they do business across boundries with partners and suppliers."
- Jim Manzi

Stop a minute. Think about our industry. Think about all the changes in the past few years. The rate of change in the investment management field has been nothing short of phenomenal. And nowhere is the rate of change faster than in the affluent market sector.

Let's fast forward a few years, and see where all the change is taking us.

"A toast. To a new era," said Robert Opel to his friends and family at 12 midnight December 31, 1999. It's the turn of the century and life has changed dramatically in the last few years. This is especially true for the investment management business.
The next day, Robert was communicating with the fee-based investment advisors with whom he shares a B-net.[1] "To think, less than two years ago there wasn't even a B-net for independent advisors. Now all of us can conduct our business less expensively and more efficiently, than the top wirehouses could five years ago."

"And five years ago there were about eight very large national wirehouses," added Betty Landon. "Now there are only three. And they're not what they once were. It's not only the brokerage business that's been consolidating, so has the insurance industry and the mutual fund industry. There are

fewer, bigger companies."

"It's the technology," Kenneth Beldan chimed in. "The technology made it all possible. It made it so that we can have our own proprietary intranet and work with fund companies and money managers and service companies on a level that makes us as competitive as the best wirehouses ever were. Each of us can deliver as good products and services as the largest money managers. Besides, the pay is better, and you're your own boss."

"It's that and more," said Robert, "with all the technology, for my clients, it's still me they are doing business with. We're in the relationship business. We can work those relationships as well as anyone out there when it comes to upscale markets. Besides, they're looking for the expertise, the value we provide. The pension business and the retail business is dominated by the big players who can make it work with such poor margins. For us, the affluent investor who's looking for someone to be there and provide not only service, but education—that's our client."

Betty added, "The nice thing about it all is that it's just going to get better. And with that, gentlemen, I have to shift–one of those affluent investors, a client, is about to connect."

We see this financial transformation beginning to emerge today. Structural drivers are reshaping the industry, forcing large firms to consolidate at one end of the market and open up opportunities for independent investment advisors at the other. A change of this order of magnitude certainly qualifies as a "paradigm shift".

The word paradigm comes from the Greek. It means "model". So, a paradigm is a model or representation of the way things work. A paradigm shift occurs when one model is replaced by another model. The classic example of a paradigm shift is when the model of the sun, moon and stars, in orbit around the earth, was replaced by the new paradigm of the earth circling the sun. Thomas Kuhn developed the notion of paradigm shift in his revolutionary work in the field, <u>The Structure of Scientific Revolutions.</u>[2]

Exhibit 4.1 THE TRADITIONAL AND EMERGING INVESTMENT INDUSTRY PARADIGMS COMPARED

Factor	Traditional Investment Industry Paradigm	Emerging Paradigm
Market	Concentration of wealth	Wealth widely distributed
Technology	Mainframe oriented; users had to be concentrated	PC based; users can be anywhere
Investment Information	Known to an elite set of advisors	Available to wide range of advisors
Concentration	Minimum size of firm for critical mass	Very large and very small firms compete effectively

The paradigm we are considering is the way investment management services are provided to the affluent. When you hear of a management consultant or training specialist or coach talk about shifting your paradigm, they are saying you should think about how you're running your business and do things differently. Just as in science, a paradigm shift happens when scientists rethink fundamental theory and begin to do their science differently. A paradigm shift is an evolution of ideas. You do not make a paradigm shift happen; instead, you recognize external changes that are making a paradigm shift happen. If you recognize the evolution of external changes, you can then take advantage of them.

This change has come about so suddenly, we can all remember the old investment industry paradigm. The old, or traditional, investment industry paradigm involved concentrated wealth in the hands of an elite, served by a set of high end investment advisors. These advisors worked for institutions, because the back-office technology was computer mainframe oriented. There were few small investment advisory firms because a critical size was required to adequately serve clients. Client loyalty was directed at the institution; institutional loyalty was often inherited along with the trust funds (Exhibit 4.1).

There is, however, a new investment world paradigm. It has come about because of technological, demographic, political, socio-cultural, and economic forces. Since the Second World War, and especially during the coming of age of the baby boomers and their over-funded 401(K) plans, there has been a boom in affluence, and the new rich are different from the old. The new rich distrust institutions. Computer technology now makes it possible for a mainframe to be housed in a PC. Put all of this together, and the paradigm shift to independent investment advisors seems somehow inevitable. The paradigm shift in the investment management industry is that affluent clients are no longer dependent on institutions and their representatives for investment advice. Because of all these external changes in our industry, affluent clients can now obtain investment advice from independent investment advisors who, in turn, obtain resources from institutions.

Because of the paradigm shift, investment advisors no longer must rely on the wirehouses. Instead, they can go off on their own. Breaking out of the wirehouse environment and setting up shop on their own is a growing trend that may very well accelerate in the coming years. At the same time, the brokerage firms are coming to recognize this paradigm shift and are taking steps to maintain their producers. They, like all the financial institutions, are looking to win the loyalty of investment advisors.

There is an very important perspective on the paradigm shift we can tap into. It is the perspective of independent investment advisors themselves. What are the drivers producing this paradigm shift? What is occurring in the environment that is fueling the growth of independent investment advisors? What was important to independent investment advisors in their decisions to break out?

To get the answer, we polled 341 independent investment advisors and asked them to what was important to them in their decision to become independent. Six answers emerged; here they are:

- **Technology:** the same technology, once only available within institutions, is now available to independents.

- **Clients:** affluent investors want customized, sophisticated investment advice and are looking for trusted advisors.

- **Products:** the commoditization of products makes them easy to obtain from many institutions.

- **Compensation:** the opportunity to earn higher income than is possible working for a financial institution and the opportunity to build equity in a business.

- **Flexibility:** the opportunity to provide any investment product an affluent client needs instead of being restricted by a financial institution.

- **Entrepreneurship:** The opportunity to utilize creative management skills in my business, instead of following the rigid policies of a financial institution.

Let's begin by examining each of these drivers in more detail.

The way independent investment advisors think is critical to their decision to be independent. That is, the way they approach business — their entrepreneurial orientation as well as their focus on meeting affluent client needs — is a strong defining characteristic on independent investment advisors.

Technology

First and foremost, it is advancements in technology which are what makes it possible for investment advisors to be independent. Yes, investment advisors want to be entrepreneurial. Yes, they desire to be client-focused. Yes, the affluent market is growing and is seeking high-quality investment advisors. Yes, all investment products are commodities. Yes, investment advisors prefer to be paid more, which is possible, because they are independent. However, if it were not for the advances in technology, being independent would be an impossible option for investment advisors.

Without the recent breakthroughs in the speed at which data can be processed, the evolution of data networks and the fall in the cost of data storage, it would be not be possible for investment advisors to work for themselves. The cost of providing the technological infrastructure would be far beyond the resources of the vast majority of independent investment advisors. In addition, if it were not for the technology, financial institutions would be unable to provide the support that enables independent investment advisors to be competitive.

Exhibit 4.2 SIX REASONS WHY ADVISORS GO INDEPENDENT

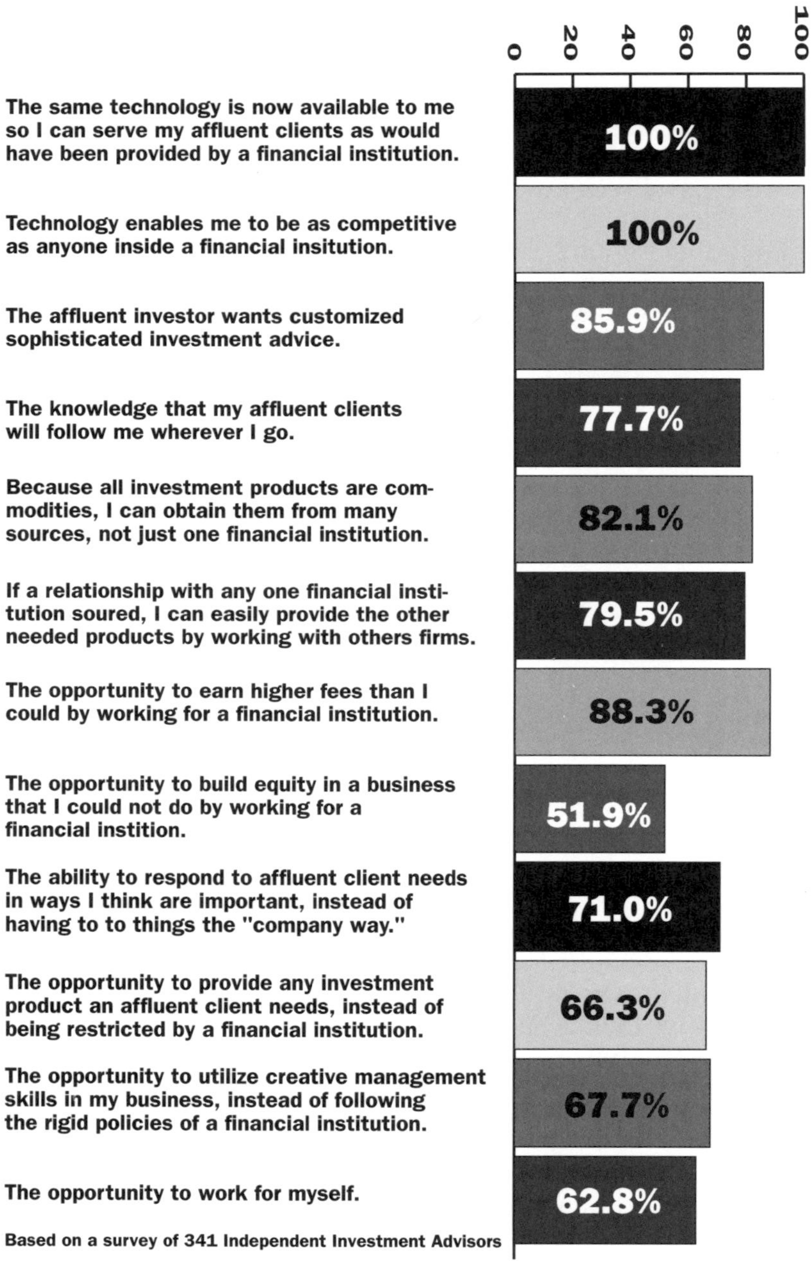

Independent investment advisors clearly understand the role technology plays in their ability to be independent. All (100.0%) said that the same technology is available to them so they can serve their affluent clients as would have been provided by a financial institution. All (100.0%) reported that technology enables them to be as competitive as anyone inside a financial institution.

What has happened is that investment advisors are outsourcing many functions. What is left tends to be more keenly focused on building a business. Selling and relationship management, portfolio management for some, and investment product selection for others, as well as managing the practice, are the activities independent investment advisors do particularly well.

Clients

The investment management business is growing. That is, more and more assets are searching for high-quality professional management. This trend covers the spectrum from retail to institutional clients. This trend is especially pronounced in the affluent investor segment.

Moreover, investment advisors recognize that affluent investors recognize the need for the advisory services they provide. Specifically, most independent investment advisors (85.9%) believe that affluent investors want customized sophisticated investment advice. Thus, the advisors see opportunity. This translates into a sense of confidence in the future of their businesses, and a successful future as an independent.

Another aspect of market demand is an understanding of who "owns" the well-to-do client. Part of the decision to go independent was predicated on the belief that affluent clients will follow them. Nearly four out of five of the independent investment advisors (77.7%) felt extremely confident that their affluent clients would follow them as opposed to staying with the financial institution where they were previously affiliated.[3] Thus, the quality of their interpersonal as well as professional relationships with affluent investors was a critical factor in the decision to go independent.

Products

In the final analysis, any investment product an investment advisor is delivering is a commodity. Without question, some investment products perform better than others. Some are more esoteric than others. Some are even nearly unique — at least until another financial institution creates a knockoff. Nevertheless, at their core, all investment services and products are commodities. They are a way to manage money. From the perspective of the investment advisor, they are commodities for two reasons.

One, there are other very similar investment products that can be accessed. Hence, if an investment advisor wants to use a value mutual fund, he or she has a number from which to choose. And from that number, a percentage are performing similarly well. This translates into a decreasing reliance on the products of any specific financial institution. Most independent investment advisors (79.5%) reported that if a relationship with any one financial institution soured, they could easily provide the investment products they needed by working with other firms.

Two, most investment products one investment advisor can sell can be sold by another. For many investment products, affluent investors can obtain them from any number of sources. A significant number of independent investment advisors (82.1%) see this and they know they are not tied to a single financial institution.

As investment products are commodities, what the investment advisor is providing is expertise. Expertise is specifying the investment needs of affluent individuals. Expertise is selecting the right investment products. Expertise is ensuring that the affluent client's investment needs are being met over time.

Compensation

If you work for a brokerage house, there is a cost — think of it as a franchise fee. This is what you pay the wirehouse for the support services they provide. The fees range from 40% to as much as 60% or 70%. However, there are some regional brokerages that are willing to take a smaller fee but they will provide fewer services.[4]

The same arrangement is true for fee-based investment products within the insurance industry. If an agent uses the insurance company's broker/dealer there is also a cut that goes to the firm. Moreover, there is often a slice for the general agent as well. In effect, the insurance agent providing fee-based investment management services is sharing the revenue with others.

When producers are independent, all the fees go to them. As a result, there is a big difference between the money an independent producer grosses and the money an affiliated producer grosses. This difference in compensation is one of the main factors making being an independent investment advisor so attractive; 88.3% rated this factor as being extremely important.

Along similar lines, but to a lesser degree, 51.9% of independent investment advisors are attracted to the idea of building equity in a business. Building equity in a privately held business is not possible if the advisor is working for a financial institution. The idea of equity in an investment advisory firm is attractive because there are opportunities to capitalize by selling your position in the firm or selling the firm outright.[5]

Flexibility

For years there has been talk in the investment management business about being client-oriented. There has been just as much talk about just what it means to be client-oriented. It's a question that still persists. We say that being client-oriented is about doing an exceptional job for the client. Being client-oriented is about identifying clients' needs and wants and taking steps to meet those needs and wants.

One of the major frustrations for investment advisors in the 1980s and into the early 1990s were limitations placed on them by the financial institutions in which they worked. Many investment advisors felt they were being limited in what investment products they could provide to affluent clients and prospects. Nearly two-thirds of the independent investment advisors (66.3%) said they were attracted to the opportunity to provide any investment product an affluent client needs instead of being restricted by a financial institution.

Investment advisors were also frustrated by their inability to be flexible in prospecting. Many felt hemmed in by the activities of compliance officers. Not surprisingly, quite a few (71.0%) investment advisors identified the ability to respond to affluent client needs in a way they think is important instead of having to do things the "company way" as being a significant factor in their decision to be independent.[6]

The concept of being client-focused has dramatically altered the way independent investment advisors are now working with financial institutions. More precisely, it is a major determinant of which financial institutions they will work with as well as what they expect from these firms.

Entrepreneurship

One of the distinguishing characteristics of successful independent investment advisors is their entrepreneurial orientation. It does not matter if they are independent or work for a financial institution. They are entrepreneurs. The majority (62.8%) find the opportunity to work for themselves instead of a financial institution to be particularly attractive.

What also makes independent investment advisors entrepreneurs is their problem-solving approach to working with clients. Of the 341 independent investment advisors surveyed, 67.7% said that they wanted the opportunity to be creative in how they manage their business instead of having to follow the policies of a financial institution.

The Resource Warehouse—Distribution Distinction

The single most dramatic result of the paradigm shift is the resource warehouse - distributor distinction. Until recently, this was not a meaningful distinction. The broker distributed the investment products that were manufactured by the brokerage firm. Today, the world of the new paradigm is very different. The resource warehouse - distribution distinction is emerging a very important (perhaps even dominant) structure (see Exhibit 4.3).

Under the traditional paradigm, it was necessary for an investment advisor to be employed by an institution in order to have access to critical resources, including products, back office systems and value-added services. Under the traditional paradigm (shown above) the distribution system of investment advisors was contained within the financial institution holding

Exhibit 4.3 OLD AND NEW RESOURCE WAREHOUSE PARADIGMS

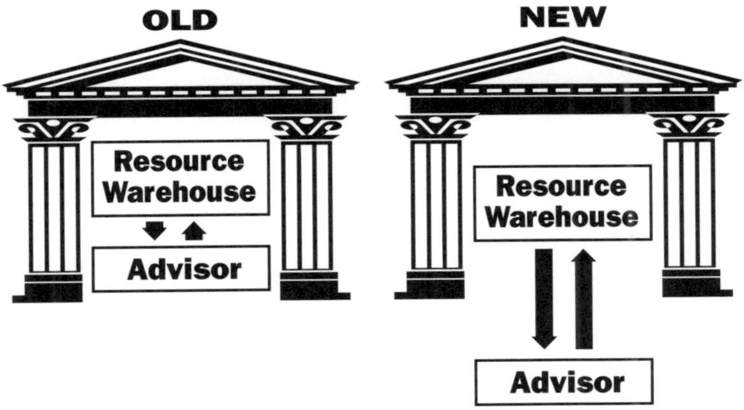

the resources. Under the new paradigm, distribution and resource warehouse functions can be separate. Institutions continue to create resource warehouses.[7] Resource warehouses are the creators and collectors of investment management products and services which range from mutual funds to discretionary investment accounts, variable products, information used by investment advisors to construct portfolios, and back-office support services.

Today, under the new paradigm, the distribution system of investment advisors can be independent of the resource warehouse. Not only that, but because of technology, the distribution system can access the investment management services and products of not just one, but a great many different resource warehouses. For instance, due to the mutual fund supermarkets that exist today, an independent investment advisor has available thousands of funds to choose from, most without loads or transaction costs.[8]

Under the new paradigm, even these distinctions become blurred. What was once solely a distribution system can now also be the resource warehouse. Consider the case of the independent investment advisor providing services as a portfolio manager. For those independent investment advisors who manage money themselves, the technology exists to permit them to, with relative ease, handle the administrative matters as well. Moreover, the technology permits them to access information they need on which to base their investment decisions.

Investment Advisors Rule

What is the bottom line when it comes to the resource warehouse—distribution distinction? Under the new paradigm, the power in the investment management business lies in the distribution system. The investment advisor — the professional with the relationship with the affluent investor — is increasingly in control. Under the new paradigm, investor loyalty vests in the investment advisor, not the institution.

If you consider the commodity nature of investment products, it is apparent that under the new paradigm, this is a business of relationships, not product features or institutional aura. From the perspective of the independent investment advisor and their affluent client, if it isn't a growth fund from ABC, then it's a growth fund from XYZ. Under the new paradigm, there are so many similar investment products out there with comparative track records, philosophy and talented portfolio managers, that an independent investment advisor always has many to choose from.

The new paradigm has significant consequences for institutions. We find that some institutions persist in thinking of the affluent investor as their client even though they market their investment products through independent investment advisors. This is a short-sighted view.[9]

The situation for financial institutions is further complicated by the growing number of them.[10] Some financial institutions have responded to the new paradigm by refusing to become a resource warehouse, that is, by refusing to offer their products and services to independent advisors. However, this has proved to be no brake on the growth of the independent investment advisory system. Independent investment advisors have available to them more than enough alternatives to offer their affluent prospects and clients.

Under the new paradigm, institutions are searching for ways they can retain their own captive distribution systems and, at the same time, offer products and services to the independent advisor. This is a difficult balancing act. For now, independent investment advisors are in a powerful and influential position, and are emerging as one of the most effective distribution systems available today.

Going Forward

- The old paradigm of institutional power in the financial services market has been replaced by a new paradigm.
- Under the new paradigm, independent investment advisors emerge as the new power, because affluent clients are loyal to them.
- There are six reasons for the emergence of the new paradigm. They are:
  - –Technology: the same technology once only available within institutions is now available to independents.
  - – Clients: affluent investors want customized sophisticated investment advice and are looking for trusted advisors.
  - – Products: the commoditization of products makes them easy to obtain from many institutions.
  - – Compensation: the opportunity to earn higher income than possible working for a financial institution and the opportunity to build equity in a business.
  - – Flexibility: the opportunity to provide any investment product an affluent client needs instead of being restricted by a financial institution.
  - – Entrepreneurship: The opportunity to be creative in how business is managed instead of having to follow the policies of a financial institution.
- Under the new paradigm, resource warehouse functions of the investment institutions have become separated from the distribution functions, creating conditions which foster the growth of independent investment advisors.

$

[1]B-nets are very common in the year 2000. They are proprietary intranets. In this case, a number of independent investment advisors are able to easily share information with each other as if they all worked for the same company. Outsiders, those not part of the group, are not able to access the network. In addition, the advisors are able to conduct aspects of their business over the B-net. Such networks have provided them with the resources to compete with other money managers much larger than themselves.

[2] Kuhn, T.S. The Structure of Scientific Revolutions, Chicago:University of Chicago Press 1970.

[3] This perception is quite accurate. That is, independent investment advisors are indeed pulling their clients from their previous affiliation.

[4] This appears to be a growing trend. More and more brokerage houses are looking to create environments where brokers are given a lerger percentage of the revenues they generate. At the same time, the brokers are responsible for a larger percentage of their expenses.

[5] With a booming stock market and the growth of the affluent investor market, investment advisory firms are selling at a premium. To make such a deal work for you requires not only an established organization, but a well designed integration plan. Because of the way such deals are usually structured, the quality of the integration plan can make the difference between vacationing around the world and staying at only five star hotels and taking the occasional trip to a theme park.

[6] Without question, compliance is extremely important. The question is the extent to which compliance proves to be detrimental to conducting business. For example, while compliance is certainly a serious concern for a brokerage firm with thousands of brokers, the upscale broker is being handcuffed because the brokerage firm needs to create compliance procedures that are based on the "lowest common denominator."

[7]Credit for the term "resource warehouse" belongs to Charlotte Beyer, founder of the Institute for Private Investors.

[8] The mutual fund supermarket concept is also being adopted by a number of the wirehouses and broker/dealers of insurance companies. There are two reasons for this. One is that a significant number of affluent investors want the menu. The second reason, and the more important factor, is that in order to be competitive with independent investment advisors, such a strategy was necessary. Independent broker/dealers will increasingly be

going this route in order to meet the needs of independent investment advisors. See: 1997 Survey of Independent RIAs.

[9] When trusts services are involved and the financial institution is named trustee, the assets are indeed 'locked up' with the institution. Moreover, the management of the assets , depending on the trust document, may have to stay with the financial institution.

[10] For example, there are over 8,000 mutual funds from which to choose. Furthermore, most anyone can set up a mutual fund and more of those anyone's are doing so. What is happening is that the number of portfolio managers is growing. Each of these portfolio managers is interested in attracting clients. Thus, they are looking for distribution systems and independent investment advisors are, undeniably, one of the very best distribution systems available today.

5

Brokerage Firm Break Outs

"The love of wealth is therefore to be traced, as either a principle or accessory motive, at the bottom of all that the Americans do."
- Alexis de Toqueville

"It has often taken 1000 years for the standard of living to double in the most advanced countries, yet it may double for the world as a whole in the next 20 years."
- Sir John Templeton

Brokers are right in the middle of the paradigm shift. Brokers live in the midst of massive industry changes. A sizable portion of the people who are now registered independent investment advisors used to be brokers. Conversations like this one are becoming more and more common among brokers...

Over lunch one afternoon, Dale Permut said to Willa Levy, "Why are we working so hard and giving so much of it away?" Willa responded, "That's the way the system works."

"That doesn't mean we have to go along with it," said Dale, "We both know there are other ways we can run our businesses. You know they are our businesses, not the firm's."

"You do not know how hard it is to go it alone," said Willa, "I am not sure that you end up with any more money in your pocket when all is said and done."

"Have you ever run the numbers?" asked Dale.

"No," responded Willa, "but it just seems like an awful lot of work to be independent."

"It is an awful lot of work," agreed Dale, "but you get an awful lot more money at the same time."

Tom Jessup came into the restaurant and sat down, "Sorry I'm late guys. I was on the phone to a big hitter."

After Tom ordered, some small talk and a little office gossip, Dale asked Tom, "You make more than both of us combined. Have you ever thought of going independent?"

"Every once in a while. The way things are, I'm never going to break out. It doesn't make any sense for me. I use too many of the firm's resources in my business. Recently, I had a senior healthcare analyst, Victor Galleani, talk with a prospect for a managed money account. Thanks to Victor, I have the account. Over the years, I've also had the opportunity to leverage the firm's reputation and network. I look at the money they make on me as money I wouldn't be able to make on my own."

"You're different from Willa and myself," said Dale. "You're doing all sorts of things, including some investment banking deals. We are in managed money, pure and simple, and I'm not sure we're getting our fair share. Willa thinks going independent isn't worth it. I'm not so sure. I figure I'm going to have to either make a move pretty soon or just decide to sit it out. The deferred compensation program the firm is pushing looks like a set of golden handcuffs to me. Before I put on the handcuffs, I want to make sure I'm doing the smart thing."

It used to be the case that brokers dissatisfied with their arrangements with one brokerage firm would move to another. They can still do that. But many are examining a new option. That option is to go independent — to break out.[1]

Not only are brokers breaking out of their own brokerage firms, they are breaking out of the traditional brokerage industry structure. As independent fee-based investment advisors, they are in the same business they were before, often with the same clients. Only this time, they are keeping the monies they would otherwise hand over to the wirehouse. The question brokers are asking is, "does the brokerage house offer sufficient compensating value for the split they receive?"

The split is the 40%, 50%, and more often the 60% that the brokerage house gets of the revenues their brokers generate. These funds are needed to run the firm. These funds offset administrative costs, costs of recruiting and training new brokers, developing new products, positioning the firm and its brokers, and so forth.

Fee-based investment advisors have tough choices to make. Brokers who do investment banking deals or who are involved in selling new issues are less conflicted. But the broker who is a fee-based money manager, or who wants to be, has a set of hard choices to make.

Breaking Out

Brokerage firm break outs are more common now than ever before. The break out trend is on the upswing. More and more brokers are going out on their own instead of just switching firms. Not only that, it appears that the trend is picking up speed. The break out threat is significant for wirehouses, because when brokers leave, they generally take their book of business along with them.[2] That's because the primary relationship with the client has been nurtured by the broker and not the firm.

Why Brokers Go Independent

To better understand the break out phenomenon, we researched broker's motivations for going independent, for breaking out (see Exhibit 5.1). We polled 331 brokers who left their wirehouses and went independent within the last three years. Each broker we talked to manages at least $40 million for affluent individuals on a discretionary basis.

Nearly all the brokers (98.8%) believed that they could go independent and be more competitive. This is due to the advances in technology as well as the decreased restrictions (66.5%) many felt they would have working with affluent clients. In addition, about two-fifths (43.5%) felt that they could serve their affluent clients better because they had access to a wider range of investment products.

Furthermore, the brokers concluded they had an affluent client base that was loyal to them (79.8%). Thus, they expected that when they went independent, their affluent clients would go with them. This proved to be the case.

Proof of the ability to go independent and be successful came from their peers. Nearly nine out of ten of the brokers surveyed (88.8%) reported that they knew of other brokers who went independent and were successful.

A key reason for brokers to break out has to do with their perception that the brokerage firm is not doing very much for them. The great majority (91.8%) are dissatisfied with their previous brokerage firm. They do not believe that the brokerage firm is adding value (90.3%).

Finally, about half the brokers (52.6%) very much liked the idea of having an equity stake in their business. They wanted to be the boss.

Exhibit 5.1 REASONS BROKERS HAVE GONE INDEPENDENT

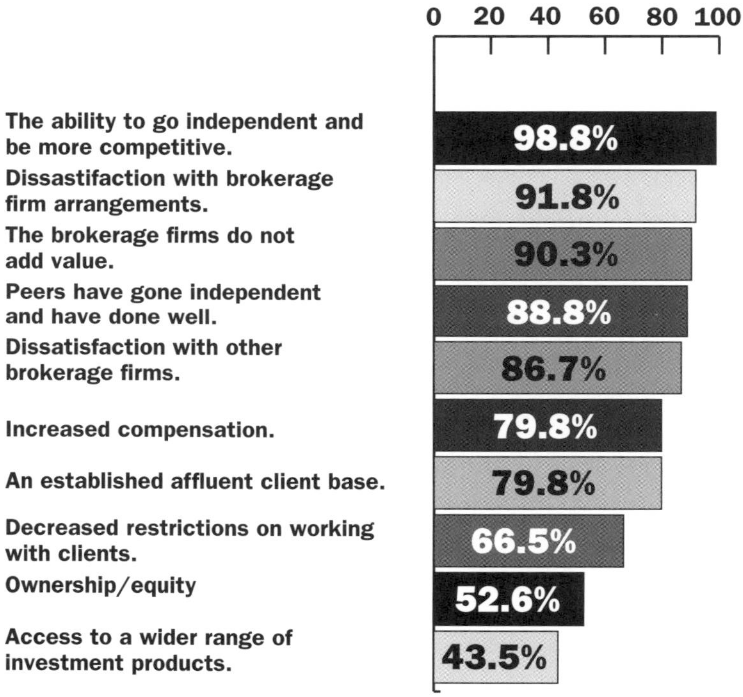

Based on a survey of 331 Brokers who went independent

The Attraction of Independence

While there is strong anecdotal evidence for the future of the break out phenomena, just how pervasive is the trend likely to be? To address this question, we surveyed 432 brokers who are each managing $50 million or more for affluent individuals on a discretionary basis. The monies are being managed personally by the broker or they are in a Wrap account of some sort. Either way, the assets are all in fee-based accounts.

Of those surveyed, 12.3% are doing serious thinking about leaving their current brokerage firm and either joining an already established investment firm or going off on their own (See Exhibit 5.2). Another 46.7% are giving it some thought; that's 59.0% or six out of ten brokers who are mulling over their options. Brokers who say they are thinking seriously about breaking out estimate that within a year they will no longer be with their current broker/dealer.

Exhibit 5.2 THE ATTRACTION OF INDEPENDENCE

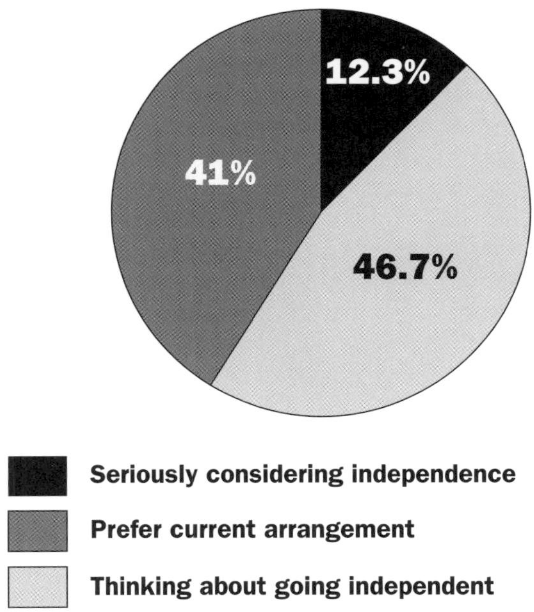

Based on a survey of 432 Brokers

Still, 41.0% of brokers prefer their current arrangement. For them being a broker with a wirehouse either provides more opportunities or more rewards because of accumulated benefits. These brokers might prefer to remain with the brokerage firm because they see that the firm enables them to be more competitive.

The research shows that high-level brokers are taking the option of being independent fee-based money mangers quite earnestly. For them, it's a matter of trading off the value they get by being connected with the brokerage firm and the increased compensation and freedom they can get by being independent.

The brokers in this study are successful (as you would expect from the assets under management). Like other established brokers, they tend to be older (average age is 51 years old), male (83.1%) and have worked for their current firm for an average of 16.1 years.

We were interested if less-well-established brokers were as ready to look at the break out option. So we did another study but set the bar lower, only requiring $30 million in fee-based investment management assets(See Exhibit 5.3).

This study included 194 brokers, and they did turn out to be younger (average age is 39 years old). However, they had an even higher degree of interest in the option of being independent. About a third (31.4%) were seriously interested in being independent and an additional 40.7% were giving it some thought. In all, 72.1% of these brokers were evaluating the idea of becoming an independent investment management advisor. Just 27.9% of these brokers are not mulling over their options.

These two separate studies reveal what we hear on the street and in the offices. Most brokers with portfolios of a substantial size are finding the option of being independent increasingly attractive. They are asking questions like, "What is the brokerage firm doing for me for what they get?" "What is the right timing for a move?" and "How should I evaluate my options?"

For brokers, the issue of breaking out is clear cut. Brokers have to look at what they do and what the wirehouse does for them and weigh the costs and benefits of getting that support in different ways. Breaking out takes a lot of analysis and preparation. Brokers look at the question of value closely. Essentially, if the supportive services offered by the institution are of substantial value for their cost, there is a tendency to stay. But if brokers feel that there is low value for the infrastructure as compared to the cost, they will look more favorably on leaving.

Exhibit 5.3 THE GREATER ATTRACTION INDEPENDENCE FOR YOUNGER BROKERS

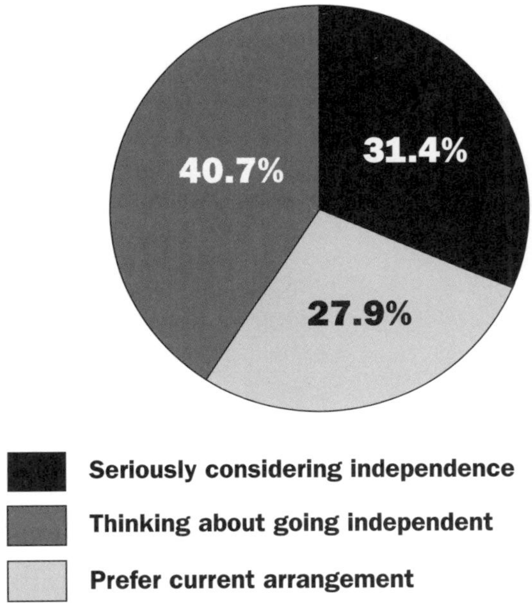

Based on a survey of 194 Brokers

We decided to look at this question of value in more detail. A survey of 956 brokers, completed in January 1997, asked detailed questions about value. A third (39.5%) of brokers said that their brokerage firm does not provide sufficient value for the percentage of the revenue they receive.

When you look at perceptions of value by number of years each broker has been in the business, the findings are more telling.

The more years a broker has been in the business, the less value they see the brokerage firm providing. Thus, they feel that the percentage of their earnings going to the brokerage firm is too much for the value they receive.

Brokerage Firms Fight Back

Brokerage firms are alert to these trends. Brokerage firms are coming to recognize the seriousness of the movement to independence, and the magnitude of the changes that this paradigm shift will mean for them. Brokerage firms are not waiting around as their best producers walk out the door. Already, many are taking steps to insure the stability of their distribution systems by actively looking to maintain their relationships with their high-level producers with beefed up support systems and revamped compensation plans.

Exhibit 5.4 JUNIORS FEEL THEY RECEIVE GREATER VALUE FROM BROKERAGE FIRMS

Years in business	% reporting insufficient value from brokerage firm	Number in subsample
1 to 3 years	12.7%	338
3 to 5 years	35.4%	291
More than 5 years	70.9%	327

At the same time, more and more firms are targeting the independent investment advisor. As a result of all this activity, brokers are becoming more aware of the choices available to them, and they are becoming more aware of their value.

Why Some Brokers Stay

Not all brokers are eager to strike out on their own. Not everyone thinks the grass (and the fee split) is greener after break out. A lot of brokers have opted to stay put. It's important to understand why.

We polled 427 brokers who were 45 years old or older and managed $30 million or more on a discretionary basis and asked about the reasons they felt tied to their brokerage firms. The number one reason brokers (who are able to break out) choose to stay instead, is because they believe the brokerage firm adds value to their practice (95.1%). The number two reason is that they believe the brokerage firm helps them to grow their businesses (91.4%). Most of the brokers (82.9%) also think the range of investment products they can offer is fine. They also disagree with the suggestion that their ability to work with affluent investors is being hampered by the firm (82.3%). Slightly more than two-thirds (70.3%) believe the compensation they receive is appropriate. That is, the split they have with the firm is acceptable for the value that the brokerage firm provides.

Some brokers (66.1%) want to stay because of the personal and professional relationships they developed with other people at the firm. These relationships are not with other brokers alone. They are also with management and support staff. About a third of the brokers (30.9%) feel the name and reputation of the brokerage firm is important to their clients, and they are proud of the affiliation.

As you might suspect, brokers this satisfied with the value provided by the brokerage houses are not likely to consider breaking out. And they do not. The idea of leaving is not attractive to this group. Nearly all (91.4%) feel that another brokerage firm is not the right way to go. About three-quarters (74.3%) see the administrative burden of being an independent investment advisor to be too much. Furthermore, more than half the brokers (54.1%) see themselves as locked-in to their firms by deferred compensation plans.

While there are a variety of reasons brokers choose to not go independent, a dominant motivation to stay with their brokerage firm is their belief that the firm adds value. That is, the association with the brokerage firm enhances the brokers' ability to grow their businesses.

Adding Value

The 378 brokers who felt the brokerage firms were getting too much were asked the likelihood that the brokerage industry will adopt a different approach to compensation and support.

Nearly all brokers who think the brokerage firm is not providing the value it could, predict brokerage firms will following regional houses, which let their brokers keep a higher percentage of their earnings while providing them less support.

Exhibit 5.5 REASONS BROKERS DO NOT GO INDEPENDENT

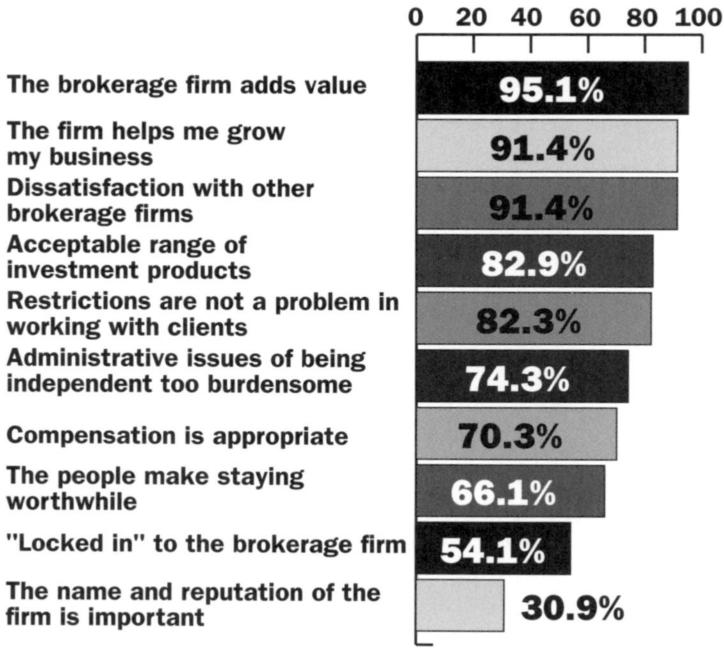

427 Brokers who have not gone independent were polled

More than 8 out of 10 of these brokers like the idea of being able to select from a menu of support services.

The brokerage firms who want to keep their high-level producers will need to add value. The brokerage firm must be able to help the brokers grow their businesses if they want their brokers to stay.

There are a number of different ways brokerage firms are doing this. One way, that is proving to be very effective, is to help brokers expand into new markets. Along the same lines, brokerage firms are helping brokers be more responsive to the needs of their affluent clients.

A clear example of this is that many brokerage firms are seeking to provide trust and estate planning services. The brokerage companies are increasingly setting up trust companies. Additionally, they are making arrangements with insurance companies to provide high-quality insurance products. Most importantly, they are setting up support systems to assist brokers to effectively offer and deliver estate and trust services. In this way, the brokerage firm is not only adding value to the broker, it is also increasing revenues for both the broker and the firm.

Another way certain brokerage firms are adding value is through their training programs. The research shows that high-level producers want training and coaching services that will enable them to incrementally grow their businesses. More often than not, this translates into programs that enable brokers to be more effective in marketing their services.

Exhibit 5.6 BROKERS PREDICT BROKERAGE HOUSE RESPONSES

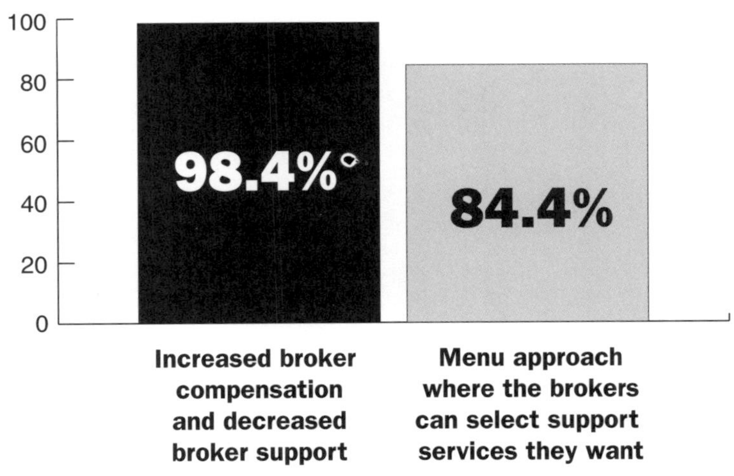

378 brokers who feel brokerages get too much

In sum, brokerage firms are recognizing the need to win over their high-level producers. Further, many firms realize they have to continue to enhance their relationship with their brokers. To the extent these firms can continue to add value, they will be able to maintain their high-level producers. In addition, they will be positioned to effectively recruit new brokers to the firm.

What's the Right Choice?

Break out? There are attractive reasons to consider the option. Most of your colleagues are re-evaluating their options, too.

Stay with the firm? A sizable number of high-level brokers choose to stay because the value the firm provides is appropriate for their percentage of the revenues the broker generates and whatever restrictions are imposed by the firm.

For the foreseeable future, there will certainly be advisors working within brokerage firms and there will be advisors who are independent. For you, or for any individual broker, the decision whether to break out or to stay with the brokerage firm will depend on your particular situation. We have provided a series of questions that can prompt your thinking on this matter further on.

Going Forward

- So many brokers have become independent investment advisors that there is a special term for the phenomenon — brokerage firm break outs.

- Brokers with significant client assets under management and younger brokers are more likely to find the break out option appealing.

- A number of brokers are dissatisfied with the level of support services they receive from brokerage houses. Those who feel they can organize the administrative and technical components of an independent practice are considering the option.

- On the other hand, many brokers are quite satisfied with the menu of support services offered by their brokerage house, and have no interest in becoming an independent investment advisor.

$

[1] Going to another brokerage firm and going completely independent are two ends of the spectrum. There is a third option which is to go quasi-independent. Regional brokerage firms in an attempt to attract high-level producers are providing this option.

[2] One way this is accomplished is by placing assets into trust. Many brokerage firms have established trust companies. For the most part, trust services have had a distinctively defensive feel. When the trust company is the trustee, the assets within the trust are, for the most part, locked-in.

6

Insurance Agents as Independent Investment Advisors

"In the future, independent financial practitioners will find a networking system mandatory to survival and client satisfaction. The group strength found in networks formed for buying power, advanced technology, and proprietary research will separate salesmen from businessmen."
- John Watts

"Managing money is not the true business of the money management industry. Rather, it is gathering and retaining assets. Good money management skills are only one of many important tools essential to the business of attracting and retaining assets."
- Mark P. Hurley, Sharon I. Meers, Ben J. Bornstein & Neil R. Strumingher

---

Brokers are not the only financial services professionals who are looking over the opportunities in investment management. Insurance agents are, too.

Greg Fromm has been an insurance agent for more than 10 years. After about a year, once he had exhausted his friends and relatives as prospects, he had found his natural market — fast food franchise owners. His uncle was a manager of a fast food restaurant and introduced Greg to his boss. From there, things slowly got going.

Now Greg is doing well as an insurance agent. In each of the last three years, he has made more than $150,000 in first year commissions. However, Greg's market is changing. Greg, like a growing number of insurance agents, is becoming increasingly interested in moving into the fee-based investment advisory business. Greg sees investment management as a natural extension of the portfolio of financial services he provides. However, Greg worries about the best way to enter this business as well as the best way to grow it.

Greg has already lost two clients to investment managers. He was most concerned about the loss of a very good client to a financial planner who provides fee-based discretionary investment management services as well as insurance. In speaking with his fast food franchise owner clients, he finds they are very interested in investment management. Greg discussed mutual funds with them, but found his clients were adverse to paying loads and preferred to work with people from whom they could obtain on-going advice.

The way the best insurance agents look at it, they already have done the hard work — they already have built up an affluent clientele. They know from experience that it is far easier to sell an existing client a new product than it is to find a new client. With the right products and services they can go back to their book of business again and again. For some insurance agents, it makes good sense to become an investment advisor in order to leverage those client relationships even further.[1]

Their instincts are right. Without question, your best clients are your existing clients. In our research of financial services we find that it is nine times easier to cross-sell financial services to existing affluent clients than it is to find new affluent clients.

Not only do high-end insurance agents have solid relationships with their affluent clients, they also have an insider's perspective on the personal balance sheet of these affluent individuals. Therefore, insurance producers reason, they can effectively position their new fee-based investment management services.

Marketing Investment Management Services

The cross-over between the insurance and investment fields has been building over the past decade. At the high end, there is a considerable overlap in the markets and products when you look at insurance agents and brokers. Increasingly, brokers want to sell life insurance and related products. Increasingly, insurance agents want to sell investment management services.[2]

In fact, over half of all insurance agents with affluent clients are interested in broadening their practice to include investment management services. We found this out in a survey of 494 high-end insurance agents (generating $100,000 or more in first year life insurance commissions in each of the last five years[3]). Most (57.1%) said they were evaluating the business case for getting actively involved in the investment management business (see Exhibit 6.1).

Exhibit 6.1 INTEREST AMONG INSURANCE AGENTS IN THE INVESTMENT MANAGEMENT BUSINESS

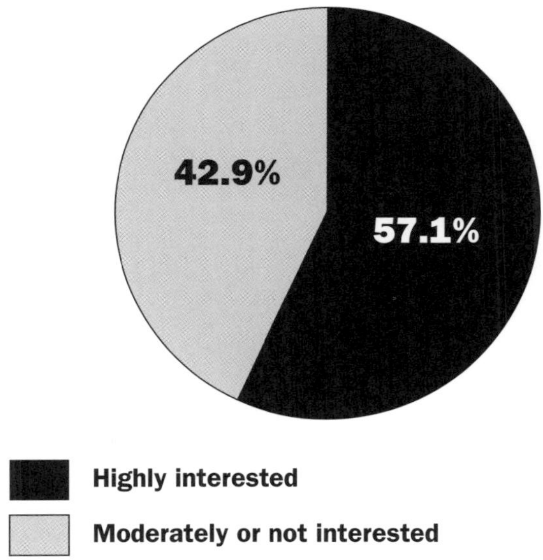

Based on a survey of 494 High-end insurance agents

Of course, some agents have been active, fee-based investment managers within the old insurance industry paradigm. But just as with brokerage houses, they no longer feel they are getting enough support from these institutions. They are looking, seriously, at becoming independent, just as brokers are. The problem for insurance agents is that they feel insurance companies are not enabling their agents to be competitive in investment management areas.[4] In a survey of 443 career agents who are already fee-based investment advisors (they make more than 50% of their annual revenue from fees on assets under management), a majority (58.2%) said that they expect to move to an independent broker/dealer within a year or two. Another quarter (24.6%) said they are seriously considering this option. The remaining 17.2% are very satisfied with their insurance company's broker/dealer (see Exhibit 6.2).

Exhibit 6.2 CAREER AGENTS WITH INVESTMENT ADVISORY PRACTICES ALSO WANT TO GO INDEPENDENT

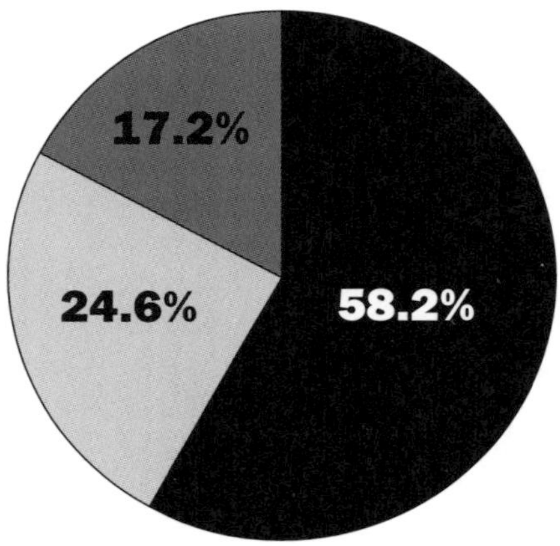

Switch to an independent broker/dealer

Seriously considering switching

Stay where they are

Based on a survey of 443 Career agents

As before, we wanted to know more about exactly why the people who moved to an independent broker/dealer did so. Were the reasons insurance agents went independent the same as those of brokers? We asked 201 high-end insurance agents (first year commissions of $100,000 or more) who left the career system and moved their book to an independent broker/dealer (see Exhibit 6.3). The single most important reason agents go independent is that they want to be more competitive with other providers of investment advisory services (97.0%). They want to compete on an even playing

Exhibit 6.3 REASONS INSURANCE AGENTS GO INDEPENDENT

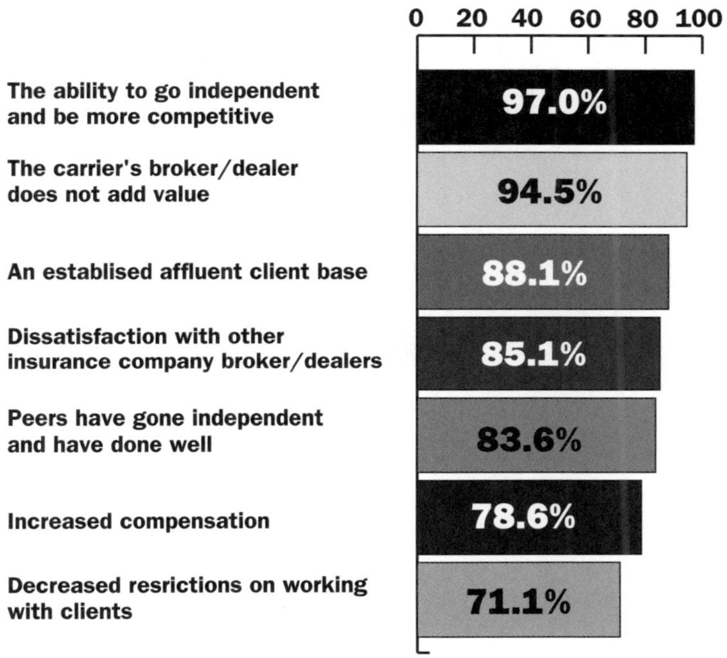

201 Insurance agents who went independent were polled

field with stock brokers, private banks, large money management firms and other insurance agents.

Insurance agents are similar to brokers in one important area. Insurance agents find the insurance company's broker dealer does not add sufficient value (94.5%). These agents are focused on fee-based business and most insurance company broker/dealers are not up to speed in this field. Insurance agents are critical not just of their company's broker/dealer, but the house broker/dealer in all insurance firms (85.1%).

Insurance agents, like brokers, also recognize that their ace in the hole is the loyalty of their clients. The agent's established clients are important (88.1%) because they will follow the agent, and insure a viable business. The agents also know that going independent can be done because their peers have done it successfully (78.6%), so the risks seem to be low. Finally,

Exhibit 6.4 YOUNGER AGENTS ARE MORE INTERESTED IN INVESTMENT MANAGEMENT

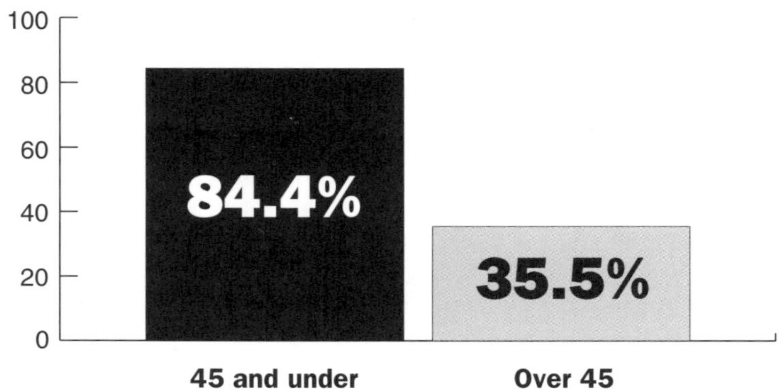

Based on a survey of 494 high-end insurance agents

71.1% said they prefer being independent because there are fewer restrictions on working with clients.

Younger insurance agents are more excited by the investment management business than older agents (see Exhibit 6.4). Agents 45 years old and younger (84.4%) are much more interested in the investment management business than agents over 45 years old (35.5%).

Younger agents tend to be more comfortable with the nature of investments. They are more likely to be excited by variable products and mutual funds than older agents. Younger insurance agents are more apt to look at variable products as a tax advantaged way of investing in mutual funds. This view is especially attractive to their business owning and professional clients (i.e., physicians and dentists)[5] who tend to share the same perspective about variable products.

The Attraction of the Investment Management Business

For insurance agents, the attraction of investment management is four-fold (see Exhibit 6.5). The reason most high-end insurance agents are interested in investment management is the profitability of the business (96.8%). It's not a secret that money management with the affluent is potentially quite lucrative, as we

Exhibit 6.5 REASONS INSURANCE AGENTS ARE INTERESTED IN INVESTMENT MANAGEMENT

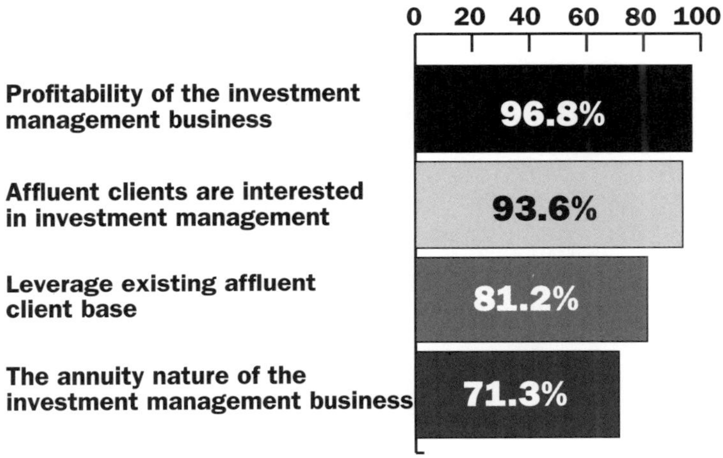

Based on a survey of 282 High-end insurance agents

discussed in Chapter One. High-end insurance agents are quick to see business opportunities.

Another major reason for the interest among high-end insurance agents is that investment management is in great demand among their affluent clients (93.6%). As brokers, banks, and independent investment advisors are, at a growing rate, offering insurance services to their affluent clients, insurance agents need to be able to offer a similar line-up of financial services. In this way, they can compete, head-to-head, with all other financial services providers.

As noted above, many high-end insurance agents (81.2%) already have a well-developed affluent clientele that can be leveraged. That is, they already have found and established high-quality relationships with affluent individuals that provide the foundation to market investment management services. Adding such services enable them to generate more business from current affluent clients that is much easier than prospecting for new affluent clients.

Exhibit 6.6 CONCERN OVER STEPS TO BECOMING AN INVESTMENT ADVISOR

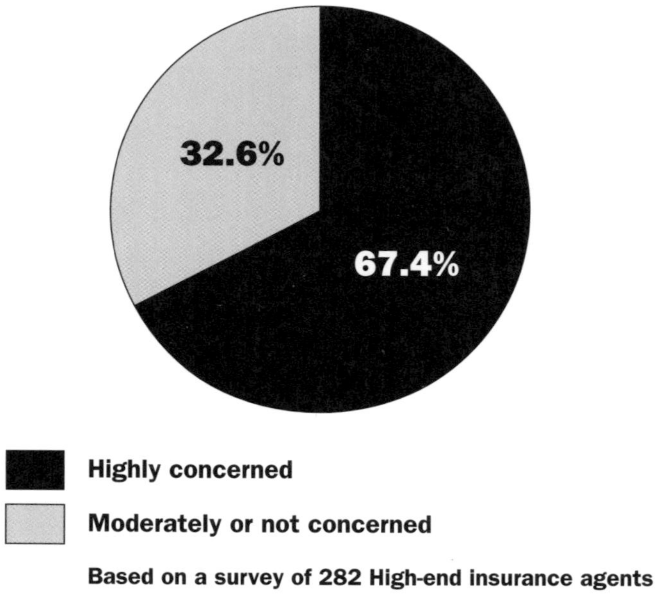

Finally, the majority of high-end insurance agents (71.3%) are attracted to the annuity nature of the investment management business. For the most part, life insurance products are front-loaded.[6] That is, all the commissions are paid when the product is sold. The front-loaded nature of the insurance business means that they must always be looking for new sales. Moreover, once a sale is made, that particular affluent client is unlikely, in the near term, to need more life insurance. Clearly, having a steady stream of revenue coming in can be very attractive. High-end insurance agents recognize that fee-based investment management services provide such a revenue stream.

Becoming an Investment Advisor

The basic hurdle faced by many insurance agents is just how to enter and work in the fee-based investment management business. Of 282 high-end insurance agents very interested in being investment advisors, 67.4% worry most about the steps they have to take to incorporate investment management services into their current business (see Exhibit 6.6).

If you are a high-end insurance agent seeking to become a fee-based investment advisor, you have a number of options. One approach is to work through your primary insurance company — the insurance company you use most. Insurance companies have broker/dealers and increasingly are setting up to accommodate successful insurance agents who want to work to provide fee-based investment management services to their affluent clients.

Another option might be to affiliate with a producer group or insurance brokerage network that is able to deliver the same services. For the most part, this currently is not a viable option as few of these organizations have put the necessary structures into place. However, as more and more insurance agents move into the money management field, producer groups and insurance brokerage networks are likely to take steps to accommodate them.

An increasingly popular option is for insurance agents to go independent and affiliate with an independent broker/dealer and/or service firm.

The structure of the insurance industry geared to the affluent markets has always been producer driven. Insurance agents, even so-called captive agents (i.e., those tied primarily to one insurance company), still have the ability to place business most anywhere. That is, they can use the products of the insurance company where they are career agents or place business with another insurance company. Just as in the brokerage industry, we see the same resource warehouse - distributor structures emerge.

Competition for Insurance Agents Turned Investment Advisors

As more and more high-end insurance agents enter the investment management business, there will be more and more institutional competition for their business. Based on these data, we would expect to see a number of insurance agents affiliate with independent broker/dealers. And, we would also expect insurance companies to try to keep their best and most productive agents.

Insurance Companies Seek to Win Over Their Own Agents

Like brokerage firms, insurance companies are very aware of the desire of insurance agents to be fee-based investment advisors. Most insurance companies already have broker/dealers. In addition, a significant number have their own investment management units. These insurance companies want to attract and retain high-end insurance agents who are interested in providing investment management services to affluent individuals.

To date, most of the focus of these insurance companies has been on providing the opportunity to sell variable products and mutual funds. However, with the trend towards customized investment management and fee-based compensation, a number of insurance companies are taking steps to assist insurance agents to work in this manner.

Some of the support services which are currently provided by insurance companies or which are on the drawing board include:

- Arranging for the insurance agent to become a registered investment advisor.
- Handling the on-going paper work associated with being a registered investment advisor.
- Assisting in dealing with compliance issues.
- Providing a range of investment vehicles.
- Arranging for advanced training.
- Providing marketing support.

This trend will place some pressures on the traditional insurance industry way of doing business. For example, the ability to act as a fee-based investment advisor is tied to the general agency system, and is likely to cause certain conflicts. In this scenario, the general agents would receive a small percentage of the fees. In such an arrangement, the question high-end insurance agents would raise is, "what value does the insurance company provide?" and "what value does the general agent provide?"

Exhibit 6.7 GENERAL AGENTS ADD VALUE

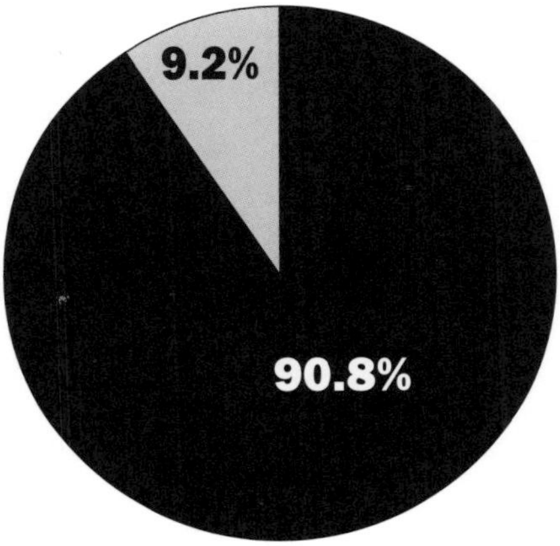

Believe general agents add moderate or no value

Believe general agents add value

Based on a survey of 282 High-end insurance agents

With respect to the general agent, there is a real question in the minds of high-end insurance agents. Most doubt that they should be part of the structure or participate in the revenue stream. Of the 282 high-end insurance agents who want to be fee-based investment advisors, very few (9.2%) believe their general agents should be involved in the process (see Exhibit 6.7).

The general agency system is currently being scrutinized as to its long-term viability. What previous research has shown was that, for the high-end insurance agent, the general agency system currently provides limited value.[7] However, if general agents can help a high-end agent enter or assist in enhancing their investment advisory business, then the agent will gladly share some of the revenue.

Conflict Over Broker/Dealer Affiliations[8]

It is becoming clear that conflicts may emerge between insurance companies and their career agency systems. There has always been some degree of stress in the system. Now, however, the conflict reaches the heart of how insurance agents work and it all revolves around the carrier's broker/dealer.

A fair number of insurance companies have also recognized that their agents want to benefit from providing investment advisory services as well. More and more insurance companies now enable their career agents to be successful in the fee-based investment management business. They are offering a wide variety of mutual funds through their broker/dealer. Some insurance companies have established Wrap account programs. A handful are looking to make more sophisticated investment products, such as hedge funds and private equity investments, available for their more experienced insurance agents to provide.

Insurance companies would prefer career agents to only use products approved by their carrier. Insurance companies would like to make it difficult or impossible for career agents to write any business outside their carriers. One way they could institute

Exhibit 6.8 CARRER AGENTS DISLIKE RESTRICTIONS ON WHAT BROKER/ DEALER TO USE

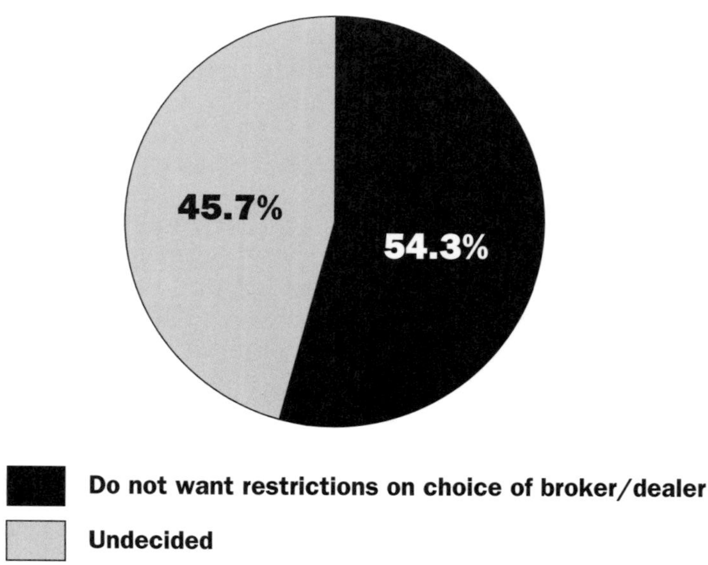

Based on a survey of 446 Career agents

this is to require career agents to use the insurance company's broker/dealer. Currently, many career agents write business with several insurance companies. Career agents like to do this because they can get a wider variety of products to meet their client needs. They also like to reduce their dependence on any single insurance company.

However, if agents have their securities license with a carrier's broker/dealer, then whatever business they do would have to go through that broker/dealer and they will be restricted to the products of that carrier. Because of the shift to fee-based investment management and the sales growth of variable products, insurance companies are requiring career agents to have their securities license with the carrier broker/dealer. They are taking this action in their self-interest. Although career agents understand why insurance companies are setting these rules, they resent being required to use the carriers broker/dealer. In a survey of 446 career agents, 54.3% said they were opposed to the insurance company requiring them using the carrier's broker/dealer (see Exhibit 6.8).

The more successful a career agent is, the more opposed they are to being restricted to the company's broker dealer (see Exhibit 6.9).

Career agents are very aware of their options in a rapidly evolving industry. The 242 career agents who are opposed to being required to use the carrier's broker/dealer would prefer to go through an independent broker/dealer (87.2%) or other similar arrangements (see Exhibit 6.10). Electing one of these options would mean being a career agent no longer.

Most (87.2%) will leave the agency system and set up as an insurance broker. They would then use any of a number of

Exhibit 6.9 MORE SUCCESSFUL AGENTS ARE MORE OPPOSED

1st year commissions	% opposed to being required to use carrier's broker	Number in subsample
Under $20,000	27.3%	154
$20,000 to $40,000	60.1%	173
More than $40,000	80.7%	119

Based upon a survey of 446 Career Agents

independent broker/dealers. There are quite a few such firms providing an entire array of products from many carriers as well as a number of value-added services. An alternative preferred by many (68.6%) is to opt for PPGA contracts with selected insurance companies. They would also turn to an independent broker/dealer for additional products and services.

Exhibit 6.10 ATTRACTIVENESS OF VARIOUS OPTIONS

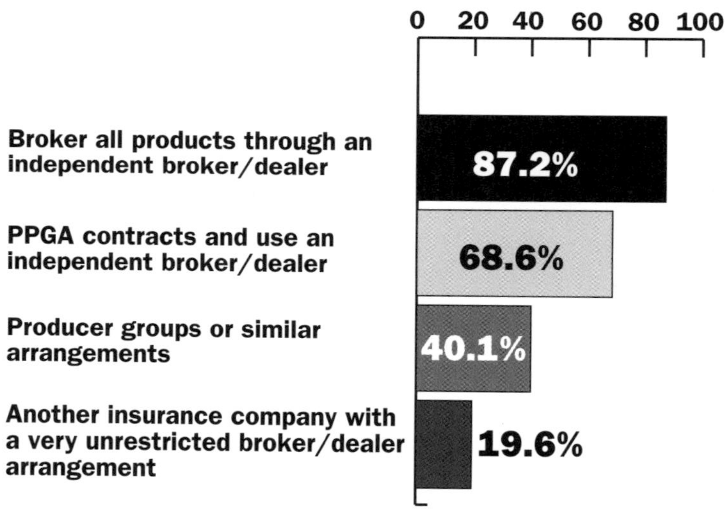

Based on a survey of 242 Carrer agents

About one in five (20.1%) would consider a producer group such as The Partners Group or the Hemisphere Group. Producer groups are using broker/dealers that support their efforts or are now setting up their own broker/dealers. Finally, 19.6% would be attracted to another insurance company if they could have flexibility to select the broker/dealer of their choosing.

It is important to keeping in mind that we are talking about some of the best of the best again. The more successful the career agent, the more easily they can switch affiliations. The career agents with the biggest established practices, are the ones most opposed to the idea of restrictions being placed on them with respect to the products and services they can offer.

Due to the structure of the insurance industry, producer groups and insurance brokerage networks must, just like the insurance companies, win the loyalty of the high-end insurance agent. Thus, they are always looking for ways to provide value added services. A major value-added service, as we have seen, is assisting high-end insurance agents position themselves in the fee-based investment management business.

Another option is for high-end insurance agents to set up on their own. Then they would market their new investment management capabilities to their existing affluent clients and target new affluent individuals for both insurance and investment management services. This way they receive all the financial benefits of being an independent investment advisor. The challenge of this option is that it requires a detailed understanding of technological and marketing requirements which are significantly different than marketing sophisticated insurance services.[9] Given the very high level of interest among high-end insurance agents, financial institutions will be creating ways to enable them to become independent investment advisors.

It's beginning to happen already. The insurance companies, the producer groups and insurance brokerage networks, as well as the free standing broker/dealers and service firms, will all be jockeying to win over the high-end insurance agent who is in or going into the investment management business. The winning institutions will be the ones who provide added value to insurance agents.

Going Forward

- Insurance agents are looking over the opportunity to become independent investment advisors by placing their licenses with independent broker/dealers.

- Many successful insurance agents are interested in offering investment management services.

- Insurance agents (independent and career agents) want flexibility in choosing their broker/dealer. Most career agents do not want to be restricted to the broker/dealer of a single carrier.

$

[1]The interest insurance agents have in the investment advisory business extends beyond just leveraging existing client relationships. For many, it's a defensive move as other financial advisors such as brokers and banks make forays into selling insurance.

[2]Prince, R.A. "Upscale Agents see Future as Fee-Based Advisors." National Underwriter, 100 (40) 1996.

[3]The insurance agents in the research program generated this income by selling life insurance to individuals. For the most part, they provide their clientele estate planning services. In other words, they are working with affluent individuals as opposed to businesses.

[4]The research shows that the more successful producers are opting to work with independent broker/dealers as well as boutique broker/dealers (many of them set up by larger insurance brokerages or insurance agent networks) and custodial firms because they can build a more rewarding investment advisory practice this way. These firms will reap the rewards of the talents of the high-end insurance agents who go independent because when they move they take their investment advisory book of business as well as their insurance business with them. Unless insurance companies take action, some of their best agents will leave because these agents have chosen to be in the investment advisory business. Insurance companies will need to dramatically rethink the investment advisory services they are making available through agents. More sophisticated Wrap Account programs are required than what is offered by the preponderance of insurance companies today. The ability to create tax-efficient portfolios is increasingly important. The integration of fiduciary services and money management will be essential. With the change in the law, the ability to evaluate and access hedge funds is going to be important. Hedge funds are no longer for institutional clients and the very wealthy. They are looking more and more like high-end mutual funds. In addition, with the change in the law, the number of hedge funds is going to explode. Hedge funds are of significant importance to insurance agents who want to excel in the investment advisory business. The ability to be able to make them available is essential for a growing number of affluent investors as well as smaller institutions. All told, insurance agents need to be conversant with hedge funds as they are already making their way into variable products. Unfortunately, hedge funds are way beyond the scope of most insurance company broker/dealers.

[5]These professionals tend to think of variable products as a tax-advantaged way of investing in mutual funds. See: Prince, R.A., Phillips, E. K., & Apolinsky, H.I. Physician Financial Planning in a Changing

Environment. CA: PMIC, 1996.

[6]The front-loaded nature of life insurance is currently in the process of being transformed. Levelized commissions as well as asset -based commissions are on the horizon. Nevertheless, at the present time, life insurance products are dominantly front-loaded.

[7]Prince, R.A. " Study Finds GAs Not Fulfilling Agents' Requirements." National Underwriter, 100 (13) 1996; Prince, R.A. " GAs at Root of Success (or Failure) of System." National Underwriter, 99 (48) 1995.

[8]Prince, R.A. "Agents Vs. Carriers on Broker/Dealer Affiliations." National Underwriter, 101 (9) 1997.

[9]Historically, high-level relationship management requirements for working with affluent clients who purchased life insurance and those who purchased investment management services differed significantly. Too often, high-end insurance agents market investment advisory services and fail to appropriately modify the way they work with affluent clients. The result is universally disastrous. Not only do these wealthy individuals pull all their business from the insurance agent, they make a concerted effort to tell all of their family, friends and peers to avoid the insurance agent. While the investment advisory business is a potential gold mine for insurance agents, to be able to mine the gold without any of the tunnels collapsing on your head necessitates being able to skillfully manage the expectations of the affluent investor. Nevertheless, high-end insurance agents have repeatedly proven that by employing relationship management strategies they not only build very rewarding investment advisory businesses, they simultaneously significantly expand their insurance practices.

7

Relationship Managers as Independent Investment Advisors

"Information about money has become more valuable than money itself."
- Walter Wriston

"Money ranks as one of the primary materials with which mankind builds the architecture of civilization."
- Lewis Lapham

Relationship managers would appear to have a natural affinity for becoming independent investment advisors. After all, they already do the job. Relationship managers are individuals whose job it is to market investment advisory services to the affluent. They are responsible for finding new clients, for selling the firm's investment advisory services and for servicing the accounts.

"Glad to see you, Robin," smiled Glenn at the MBA reunion. "How are things at the bank? Weren't you with...wait..."

"Never mind," Robin laughed, "I left them a year ago. I joined a small independent investment management firm and am having a great time."

"Isn't that risky? I mean, there's Susan and the kids, the house. Isn't going out on your own risky at your stage of life?"

"You could look at it that way," Robin responded, thoughtfully, "but it turns out there wasn't much risk at all, as almost all of my clients came with me. It turns out what they liked was working with me, not what they were getting from the bank. All I did was feel them out, found they liked the idea, and worked out the move."

Relationship managers are found in two types of money management firms. They are either employed in a firm whose primary business is providing money management services or they are employees of a private bank.[1] Because these two settings create different opportunities, let's look at them one at a time.

Relationship Managers in Investment Management Firms

Some relationship managers work within investment management firms. These firms are typically quite large; many have a billion or more dollars under management. Relationship managers in these firms have the responsibility for being the interface between the firm and the affluent client, and bringing the resources of the firm to bear on the client's financial and investment issues. In short, they already do all the things an independent investment advisor does.[2]

Since they already do much of what an independent investment advisor does, we would predict many are looking at this career option. Why, they would ask themselves, would you want to work for someone else, when you can own your own firm?

Exhibit 7.1 PERCENT OF RELATIONSHIP MANAGERS IN INVESTMENT MANAGEMENT FIRMS WHO ARE CONSIDERING GOING INDEPENDENT

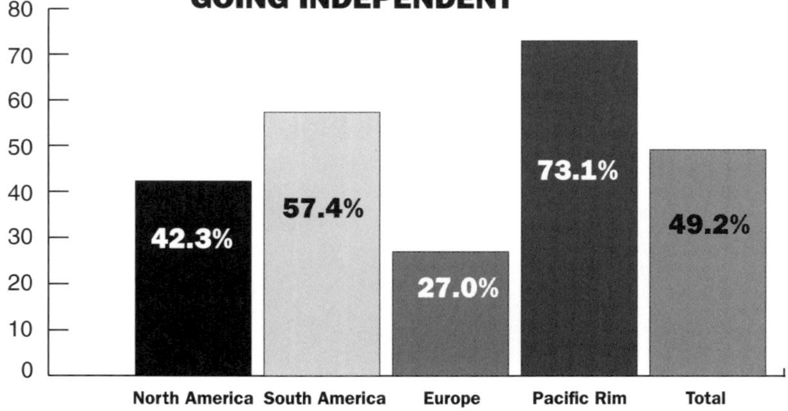

Based on a survey of 797 Relationship managers from investment management firms

That is exactly the career choice many are examining right now. In a recent poll we conducted with relationship managers currently working for investment management firms, we asked whether any were seriously reviewing their options and looking at going independent. Overall, about half (49.2%) said they are considering going independent (see Exhibit 7.1). In parts of the world, this percentage is higher (the Pacific Rim), and in other parts it is lower (Europe). In the United States and Canada, just under half (42.3%) of the relationship managers who are currently working in investment management firms are thinking of becoming independent investment advisors.

Exhibit 7.2 WHAT ATTRACTS RELATIONSHIP MANAGERS IN INVESTMENT MANAGEMENT TO THE INDEPENDENCE OPTION

Motivations	North America	South America	Europe	Pacific Rim	Total
Affluent clients will follow them	96.4%	94.4%	82.3%	93.7%	92.6%
Increased compensation	92.8%	89.9%	93.5%	92.4%	92.1%
Ownership/ equity	85.5%	69.7%	79.0%	84.2%	80.4%
Better serve affluent clients	75.9%	56.2%	72.6%	80.4%	72.7%
Peers have gone indep-endent & have done well	73.5%	64.0%	56.5%	70.9%	67.6%
Desire to be an entrepreneur	62.7%	57.3%	69.4%	67.1%	64.3%
Ability to out-source portfolio management	15.7%	25.8%	30.6%	13.9%	19.6%

Based on a survey of 392 Relationship managers from investment management firms

What attracts this group of relationship managers is how easy the move would be. Most of them (focusing on those in North America for the moment) say they are convinced their clients would follow them (96.4%). This is because they represent the firm to the client — they are the face of the firm — and the client associates the service and results with the relationship manager more than with the "faceless institution." Of course, the potential for increased compensation is not lost on these professionals. The opportunity to own one's own firm is a terrific pull as well. Perhaps, and most importantly, many know, personally, someone who has made this transition in their own practice, and been successful.

These findings will come as no surprise to institutions. They have already seen some of their best of the best seize this opportunity, and leave the firm. They know more of their relationship managers are looking over their options carefully.

You can expect institutions to react. Look for programs that tie the client more strongly to the firm, instead of to the relationship manager. Look for long term compensation agreements that knit the relationship manager more tightly to the institution. Look for more debate about non-compete agreements.[3]

Relationship Managers in Private Banks

The siren call of becoming an independent investment advisor is heard in the halls of the private banking world as well. In private banks, relationship managers are there to promote the bank's investment management capabilities, and, for some, to market a variety of services to the affluent such as trusts, credit and transaction products. Like so many other players, relationship managers in private banks have cross-over potential. That is, they already have many of the technical skills and industry know-how necessary to become independent. They also already have clients who look to them for advice and counsel.

The call is being heard. We have just completed an international study of relationship managers in private banks around the world. We asked how seriously they were considering becoming an independent investment advisor. The global average is 35.5%. One in three people responsible for client relationships within private banking circles is actively thinking about becoming an independent advisor.

Becoming independent is more appealing in some parts of the world than in others. Relationship managers in the Pacific Rim and in South America are especially likely to be thinking hard about this career evolution. Those are, of course, undergoing the most rapid transformations, so it follows that savvy professionals would want to keep tabs on all their options. The North American and Eurpoean economies are more stable, but even there, about one in four relationship managers currently employed by a private bank is weighing the pros and cons about leaving their employer and going independent (see Exhibit 7.3).

Exhibit 7.3 PERCENT OF RELATIONSHIP MANAGERS IN PRIVATE BANKS WHO ARE CONSIDERING GOING INDEPENDENT

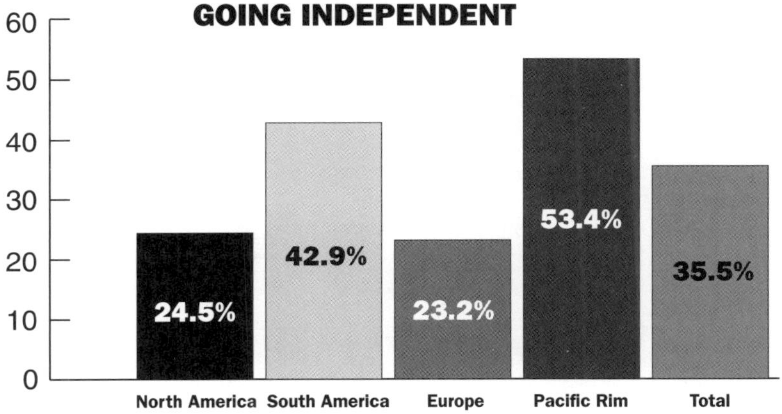

Information based upon survey of 961 Relationship Managers

Relationship managers in private banking settings have a lot of cards to play. They are very well situated to capitalize on their advantages. For example, worldwide, nine out of ten say the increased compensation is attractive, and almost as many say their clients will follow them if asked. They like the idea of owning their own company and desire to be an entrepreneur, free of the constraints of a large organization. More than half personally know someone who has made the transition to being an independent investment advisor, successfully (see Exhibit 7.4).

Attitudes in North America. follow this general trend, but are more muted. Most are certain their affluent clients will choose them over the private bank, if it came to that, and so compensation levels could be locked in. About half personally know someone who has made the jump successfully.

Here, again, the institutional side will not be caught unaware. Private banks are already alert to the threat of loosing some of their best of the best to the independent investment sector, and some of their clients besides. Private banks will be busy creating strategies to counter this strategic threat; strategies which will affect the nature of market competition.[4]

Exhibit 7.4 WHAT ATTRACTS RELATIONSHIP MANAGERS IN PRIVATE BANKS TO THE INDEPENDENCE OPTION

Motivations	N. America	S. America	Europe	Pacific Rim	Total
Affluent clients will follow them	75.0%	93.3%	63.0%	90.3%	84.8%
Increased compensation	67.6%	97.0%	80.4%	98.9%	89.4%
Ownership/ equity	63.2%	88.1%	47.8%	94.6%	79.5%
Better serve affluent clients	29.4%	31.3%	65.2%	79.6%	48.7%
Peers have gone independent & have done well	47.1%	59.7%	67.4%	77.4%	63.0%
Desire to be an entrepreneur	36.8%	82.1%	52.2%	90.3%	71.3%
Ability to outsource portfolio management	27.9%	27.6%	41.3%	14.0%	25.8%

Based on a survey of 341 Relationship managers from private banks

Going Forward

- Many relationship managers who work for investment management companies are attracted to the potential of going independent.
  - They are confident they can take their clients.
  - They are attracted to increased compensation opportunities.
- Relationship managers in private banking settings are similar.

– Many have personal role models of people who made a successful transition.

– The lure of compensation and control is powerful.

$

[1]Private bank is used here to represent all high-net-worth divisions within a bank as well as stand alone private banks.

[2]Many money management firms have the affluent client dealing directly with portfolio managers. The people we surveyed were only responsible for creating and maintaining relationship with high-net-worth investors. They were not responsible for managing the client's money.

[3]In examining the steps investment management firms are taking to hold onto their good relationship managers we find that European firms are most aggressive. This might be the reason proportionately fewer European relationship managers are interested in going independent. We anticipate more and more money management firms will be carefully evaluating ways to ensure that high-quality relationship managers stay with the firm and if they do opt to leave are not in a position to take a substantial number of clients.

[4]We do not yet observe private banks taking the same initiatives as money management firms to cement relationships with their relationship managers or with affluent clients directly. One possible explanation is that private banks have not yet fully recognized the potentially adverse consequences of their relationship managers walking out the door with a book of business. Still, we see more private banks becoming more attuned to this phenomenon and responding appropriately.

8

Accountants as Independent Investment Advisors

"Money by its very nature becomes the most perfect representative of a cognitive tendency in modern sciences as a whole: the reduction of qualitative determinations to quantitative ones."
- Georg Simmel

"Money, like number and law, is a category of thought."
- Oswald Spengler

Accountants are also moving into the investment management business. Accounting firm participation in the investment management business is not brand new. The larger firms have already moved into the field in strength. For example, most of the Big Six firms have found ways to bring investment advisory services to the high-net-worth private clients they do tax and estate planning for. Smaller and mid-sized accounting firms and solo-practitioners are getting in the act, too. Some have become independent investment advisors. Others have created relationships with services firms.

"This is the second client who has come to me with investment issues this week," sighed James Barber. James and his three partners had built up a practice principally providing services to businesses too small to have an in-house accountant. "It seems as though they are all turning fifty and are panicking about retirement and college funds for the grandkids."

"They all have retirement plans in place — right?" asked Vickie Spalding, his associate.

"Sure, put in years ago. All qualified. But they are worried abut the whole investment picture. They have been meeting with brokers and insurance agents and financial planners and reading magazines and are opinionated and confused at the same time. John actually came right out and told me he

wished I could take over the whole thing for him."

"So?"

"You know, there was a time I would have dismissed it out of hand. But I'm actually giving some thought as to how we could do a little more on the investment side. If we could, it would help the billing side of the house."

Aside from providing investment management services either directly or in conjunction with third parties, some accountants are able to collect fees for making referrals. Already in 18 states, accountants are able to receive finder's fees for referring their clients to investment managers.

Interest High; Questions Emerge

Just how much interest is there among accountants in the investment management business? It turns out to be considerable. A poll of 623 senior partners, all CPAs, of accounting firms that are not presently providing investment advice or being compensated through referrals, was conducted to answer this question. The majority (60.7%) said they were very or extremely interested in participating in the investment management business (see Exhibit 8.1).

Not only is there a high degree of interest, but many (74.3%) are already evaluating the best way to participate in the investment management business (see Exhibit 8.2).

While many issues are being considered by these firms, nearly all the accountants surveyed (91.8%) report that they do not see themselves as portfolio managers in the sense of selecting specific securities (see Exhibit 8.3). Most accountants stop short of wanting to perform the direct investment management tasks. Because of their training and professional culture, accountants generally see themselves as impartial advisors and consultants. Many do not want to be in the position of taking direct action on behalf of a client. Rather than become involved in portfolio management, accountants would prefer an advisory status, but still participate in the flow of fees.

The Appeal of the Investment Advisory Business

For most accountants (88.6%), the investment management business is appealing because their current business is not as

Exhibit 8.1 Interest Among CPAs in the Investment Management Business

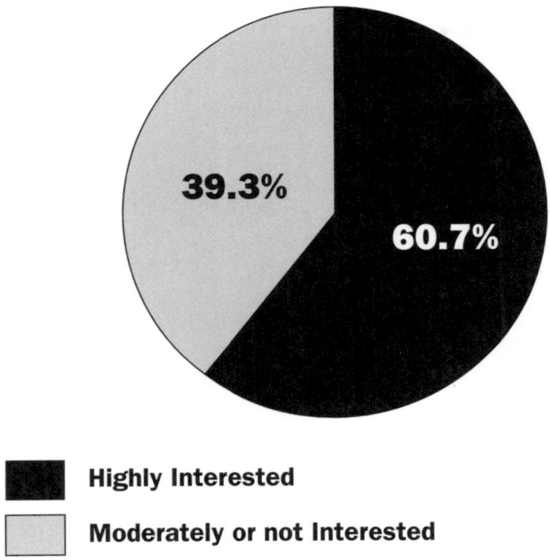

Based on a survey of 623 CPAs

profitable as it once was (see Exhibit 8.4). Accountants are coming under considerable competitive pressure for some of their core services. Tax preparation, for example, the traditional mainstay of accountants, is being displaced by computer programs and franchised tax preparation centers.

Accountants are eager to consider sources of fee income that would be an extension of their traditional business; 79.9% say they are on the look-out for such opportunities. We have already seen that competition in their usual lines of business is causing them to look around. Many have considered management and systems consulting.[1] A logical alternative is participation in providing investment management services, especially since many are moving into financial planning in one form or another.

There are other reasons investment management is a logical alternative for accountants. Accountants are the most trusted advisors that most business owners, professionals and affluent individuals have. Accountants count their relationships with their clients in decades, not years, and interact more frequently

Exhibit 8.2 THREE QUARTERS OF INTERESTED CPAs ARE EVALUATING HOW TO ENTER THE INVESTMENT MANAGEMENT BUSINESS

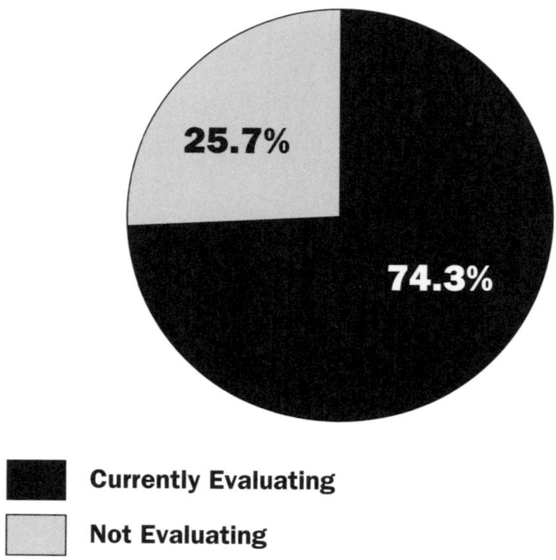

Based on a survey of 378 CPAs

with their clients than other professionals do. Impartiality, duration and frequency all foster the unusually strong relationships accountants have with their clients.[2] Most accountants (77.8%) say they can, with a high degree of effectiveness, leverage these client relationships.

Accountants acknowledge the profitability of the investment management business. Three-quarters of those we polled (75.7%) say that the financial benefits of the investment management business were significant. The annuity nature of the fee-based investment management business is appealing to all sorts of advisors — and accountants are no exception.

Nearly two-thirds of the accountants interested in participating in investment management service (64.6%), say another reason is that their affluent and business clients want the service. Affluent clients are aware of the restructuring of the investment markets, and are interested in new options opening up for them.

Exhibit 8.3 VERY FEW CPAs LOOK TO MANAGE MONEY DIRECTLY

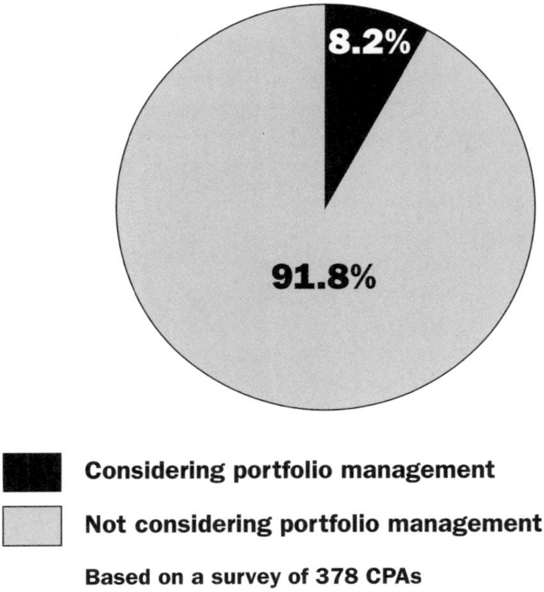

CPA Concerns

Although the case for having direct involvement in investment management would seem to be compelling, accountants raise many questions and concerns. Thus, while the majority of accountants are interested in the investment management business, and are actively exploring their options for participation, they tend to be concerned about offering investment advice (see Exhibit 8.5). Some (22.2%) are highly concerned, many (67.7%) are concerned, and just a few (10.1%) are only slightly concerned. Not a single accountant responding to our poll was unconcerned.

We probed deeper into the source of these concerns. The greatest concern centered on the possibility of damaging existing client relationships (78.8%). As we previously noted, accountants see an excellent opportunity to leverage their existing clientele. Were they to participate in investment management on any basis, they would undoubtedly approach their best clients and attempt to interest them in the additional service. Although there are the upside benefits of increased

Exhibit 8.4 REASONS INTERESTED CPAs GIVE FOR EXPLORING THE INVESTMENT MANAGEMENT BUSINESS

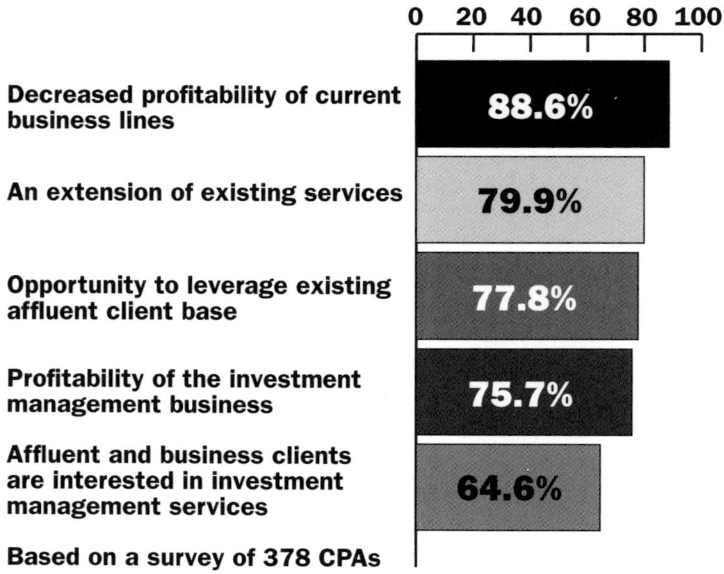

compensation, there is the significant downside of endangering client relationships. What would happen if their investment advice proved to not work out very well? Accountants justifiably worry about losing clients because of poor investment advice.

Like all professionals, accountants are also worried about personal and professional liability (61.9%). If the investment advice they provide does not work out well, being sued is a very real possibility, and is an additional point of vulnerability. Accountants also want to provide a quality service to their clients. More than half (52.6%) are concerned they may do a poor job for their clients because of their inexperience.

Accountants are conflicted about the promise and pitfalls of participation in investment management. On the one hand, many see a great opportunity in providing investment management services. On the other hand, they are very concerned about doing a good job for their clients, and worried about the risks if they do not. As a result, accountants continue to study and explore the issue.

Exhibit 8.5 THE MAJORITY OF CPAs ARE CONCERNED ABOUT OFFERING INVESTMENT ADVICE

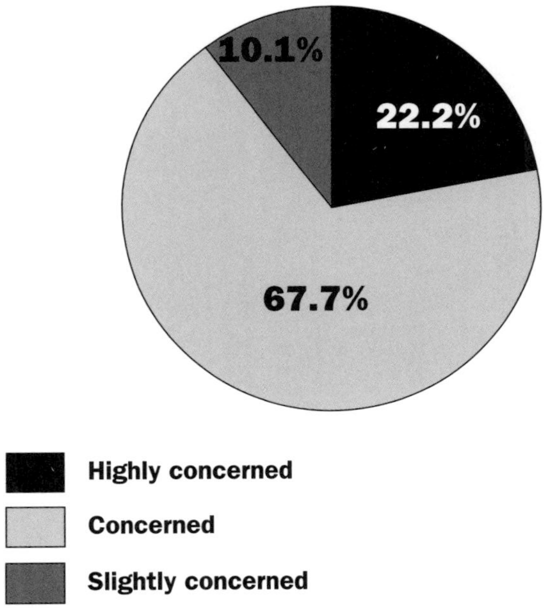

Based on a survey of 378 CPAs

There are three specific areas accountants would be interested in learning about in greater detail in order to clarify their options (see Exhibit 8.7). Of most importance to accountants is information on technical matters associated with investment management. Most (80.2%) of the accountants surveyed want more detail. Technical information refers to the basics of investment management such as modern portfolio theory.

Accountants also want to know more about the process of investment client development. They are comfortable with how things work in accounting and are comfortable with client loads and the like. In investment management, success depends on effective client development and managing more client relationships. Many accountants (58.7%) are sophisticated enough to recognize this.

Exhibit 8.6 REASONS FOR CONCERN

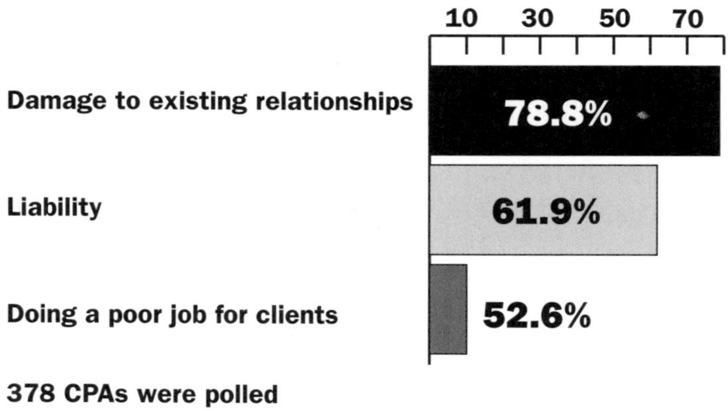

Lastly, compliance information is also considered important by 34.2% of the accountants surveyed. Accountants do not want to make mistakes in an area as important as compliance.

Investment management represents attractive opportunities for accountants, and raises concerns, too. There are a number of different directions accountants may take.

Possible Evolutions

There are as many different scenarios as there are accountants but we see four main evolutions into the future. These four probable organizational arrangements for accountants seeking to work in the investment management business each have advantages and disadvantages. The four organizational arrangements are:

- **Collect finder's fees.** Undoubtedly the easiest way for accountants in many states to be in the investment management business is to refer clients to investment advisors. In return, they could collect a finder's fee for the effort. Accountants can lower their exposure by recommending a number of investment advisors and insisting that the client makes the final advisor selection decision. However, this is not an option for many accountants, who are barred by regulations. This option also will generate less revenues than the other scenarios.

- **Establish a joint-venture with an investment advisor.** This is a relatively easy way to enter the business and generate on-going revenues. It eliminates the need to become personally proficient at providing investment management services. Fees resulting from investment management would generally be greater than finder's fees but less than direct management. In addition, control over the investment process and interactions with the client are now being shared with another professional.

Exhibit 8.7 CPAs ARE LOOKING FOR ADVICE

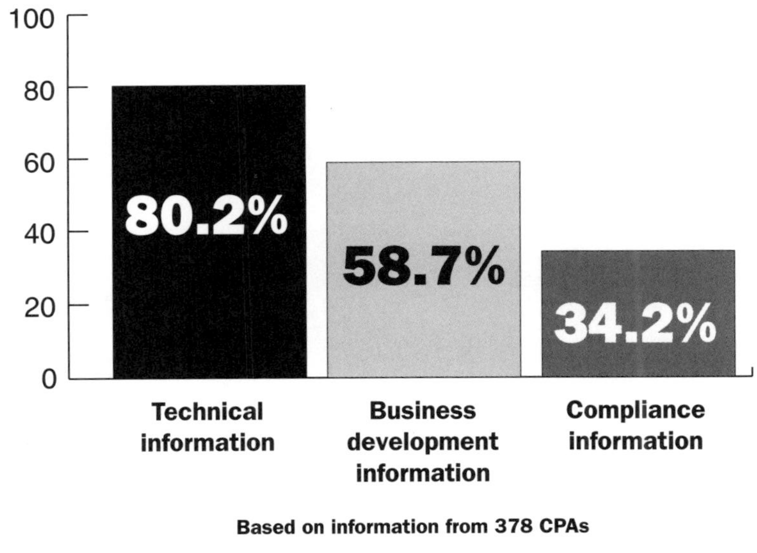

- **Use a turn-key investment management program.** Some accountants will find that they can enter the investment advisory business directly because of the ready availability of turn-key money management services. These services manage all the components in the investment management process including developing a policy statement, creating a portfolio, and portfolio rebalancing. While the accountants eventually master the mechanics of investment management, these turn-key investment management services eliminate a considerable amount of the work. If such a program is complemented by focused turn-key marketing programs, the ability of accountants to expand their business will occur quickly and be considerable. Here accountants do not have to split fees or introduce the client to other professionals.

- **Bring the requisite expertise in-house.** The most control as well as the most work occurs when the accountant brings in people to perform as investment advisors. As in the previous structure, the accountant keeps all the advisory fees. However, this organizational arrangement is initially more costly. Still, it provides the accountant with the greatest command over the process as well as the relationship with the client.

To date, all four options are being tried. Based on preliminary findings, the nature of the accounting practice and the personalities of the accountants will determine which option is best. So far, all are viable.[3]

The Question of Compensation

One of the questions accountants who are looking to enter the investment management field have to answer is how they are going to be compensated (see Exhibit 8.8). The preference is for fee-based compensation (70.6%). Very few (6.1%) are interested in being compensated for their advice through commissions. Some (8.5%) are considering a combination of fees and commissions; more (14.8%) are unsure.

Being an independent investment advisor compensated by fees is clearly the preferred choice. The rationale behind this is straightforward. Fee-based compensation will enable them to continue to be "trusted advisors" as opposed to sales professionals.

Accountants have been slow to enter the investment management business. They wait on the sidelines, attracted by the rewards but warned off because of the risks. We expect a few accountants to experiment with the business, and a few more to slowly enter as they see pioneering accountants

Exhibit 8.8 CPAS PREFER FEE-BASED COMPENSATION

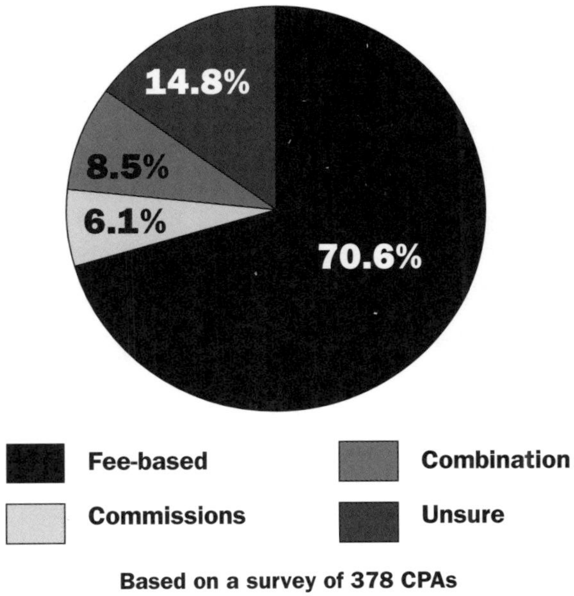

succeed. We do not see a time when accountants in general directly enter the investment management field. But, as accountants clarify their participation in investment management, there are important implications for independent investment advisors.

One important implication is that the ability of independent investment advisors to get affluent client referrals from accountants will decline as accountants become more directly involved themselves. The entry of accountants also represents another competitive force in the industry. And, accountants will be very able competitors because of the respect and loyalty they have from their clients.[4]

Resource warehouses (such as fund companies) will want to monitor developments among accountants closely. They will want to determine whether accountants emerge as another distribution system. Since distribution systems are the determining factor in gathering assets from the business and affluent markets, the resource warehouse that provides the right products and services will be positioned to win over an important emerging market segment.

Going Forward

- Like brokers, insurance agents, and relationship managers, accountants are looking over opportunities in the investment management business.

- Accountants have several advantages: frequent interaction with their clients, long-standing relationships, comprehensive knowledge of the client's financial position.

- The traditional objective and arms-length stance of accountants is a deterrent to direct involvement in money management for some.

- Accountants are finding many different ways to participate more directly in investment management.

$

[1] The large and mid-sized accounting firms have embraced management and systems consulting. For many, this aspect of their business proves to be significantly more profitable than traditional audit work. However, smaller firms have not been as aggressive in this area.

[2] Prince, R.A., and File, K.M., Marketing to Family Owned Businesses: A Toolkit for Life Insurance Professionals. OH: National Underwriter, 1996; Prince, R.A., and File, K.M. Cultivating the Affluent II: Leveraging High-Net-Worth Client and Advisor Relationships. N.Y.: Institutional Investor, 1997.

[3] The option with the highest success as measured by assets under management and satisfied affluent clients is where the accounting firm establishes a joint-venture with an investment advisor. This not only enables the accounting firm to quickly and efficiently be in the investment advisory business, it also results in more billing for the accounting firm due to increased work for existing clients as well as work for new clients. The investment advisory firms have demonstrated an ability to market both themselves and the accounting firms more effectively than the accounting firm was doing.

[4] Accountants recognize that their position of respect as a trusted impartial advisor can be seriously damaged if they assume the role of an investment advisor. Thus, we have a two-edged sword. Accountants are going to have to decide that not only are they going to be in the investment advisory business, but how involved in this business they are going to be.

9

Portfolio Managers as Independent Investment Managers

"Tell me the brand of whiskey that Grant drinks. I would like to send a barrel of it to my other generals."
- Abraham Lincoln

"The only irreplaceable capital an organization possesses is the knowledge and ability of its people. The productivity of that capital, depends on how effectively people share their competence with those who can use it."
- Andrew Carnegie

As we have seen, brokers, insurance agents, relationship managers and accountants all have close personal relationships with their affluent clients; relationships which enable them to consider becoming an independent investment advisor. There is another group with a similar sort of strategic leverage. In this case, the source of the leverage is not in client relationships but in investment expertise. Since the name of the game in investing is to beat the indices and their peers, portfolio managers who do so become hot and develop a following. With a reputation for investment talent and a client following, it is a natural evolution of a portfolio manager's career path to consider going independent.

Robert Casey is a portfolio manager. He has done quite well until now, but lately, he has been feeling that senior management is holding him back.

Rob has been ambitious; he is driven to excel, is creative, and has concern for investors. His problem is that the firm he is working for is getting in the way. He recognizes that they are not intentionally creating obstructions. On the contrary, he is certain they want him to be as productive as possible. Nevertheless, the firm is proving to be more and more of a problem.

Robert Casey, like many other portfolio managers, is

coming to realize that how they think about investment management and how their investment firms approach the business are beginning to be different. Rob knows investors are attracted to his investment style and success. He is beginning to nose around for other options.

That is exactly what is happening. Portfolio managers working in every geographic market around the globe are thinking, hard, about the risks and rewards of going independent. Worldwide, three quarters (76.6%) say they are giving it careful consideration.

In North America, the proportion of portfolio managers who are considering becoming investment advisors is 82.4%, the highest of all the geographic sectors. The relatively more open structure of the investment markets in the U.S. and Canada enables talented performers to reevaluate their position frequently. When markets undergo the type of fundamental restructuring they are now, players need to assess their position frequently. Portfolio managers have to pay attention to trends and changes in market structures, so it is not surprising that they notice changes in their own industry.

Exhibit 9.1 PERCENT OF PORTFOLIO MANAGERS WHO ARE CONSIDERING GOING INDEPENDENT

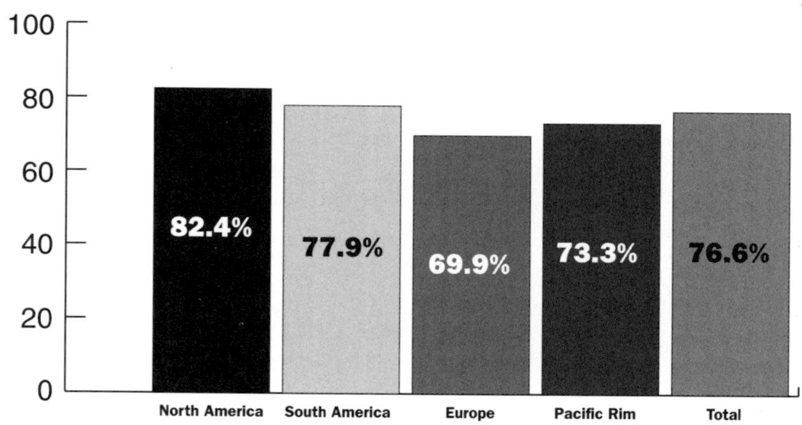

Based upon information from 368 Portfolio Managers

There are many reasons portfolio managers are attracted to the idea of being independent investment advisors. First and foremost, for North American advisors, is the appeal of being able to own their own company or to have a significant equity stake in one. Portfolio managers are typically employees, well compensated employees, but employees none the less. Because of their position in the market, they are all too well aware of the benefits to company ownership. Other appeals include increased compensation (84.7% say that is very important to them), the ability to draw investors (73.5%), greater control over their life (60.2%), and the opportunity to manage a smaller fund (59.2%).

Exhibit 9.2 WHAT ATTRACTS PORTFOLIO MANAGERS TO THE INDEPENDENCE OPTION

Motivations	N. America	S. America	Europe	Pacific Rim	Total
Ownership/ equity	90.8%	88.1%	96.1%	93.9%	91.8%
Increased compensation	84.7%	92.5%	88.2%	97.0%	90.1%
Ability to draw investors	73.5%	61.2%	62.7%	48.5%	62.8%
Greater control over own life	60.2%	74.6%	56.9%	28.8%	55.7%
Manage smaller fund(s)	59.2%	49.3%	51.0%	31.8%	48.9%

Based on a survey of 282 Portfolio managers

These appeals are not lost on investment companies. They see the threat inherent in portfolio managers breaking out. To respond to such threats, many investment companies are installing new compensation arrangements for their portfolio managers. While there is a lot of variation in how it is done, the general thrust is to create incentives for portfolio managers to stay because significant portions of their compensation are deferred and tied to the investment fund the portfolio manager is running[1].

We know of one institution where portfolio managers get significant bonuses based on their performance. However, in order to create incentives for them to stay, much of that money is placed in the fund the portfolio manager oversees. If portfolio managers stay, they will have access to the funds which (presumably) have appreciated because of their investment skills. On the other hand, if they leave, they do not get the fund.

Will these new compensation schemes deter portfolio managers from striking out on their own? The answer is, sometimes. While "golden handcuffs" are a deterrent for many, they will not be strong enough for others.

Opportunities for Portfolio Managers

So, portfolio managers are considering independent investment advisory firms. But that is not the only option open to them. Actually, independent investment advisory firms are not their first choice.

Quite a few are also considering opportunities centered on specific products such as hedge funds or mutual funds (see Exhibit 9.3). Interest in these options ranges from 52.9% to 100.0% of portfolio managers around the world. Exhibit 9.3 also confirms the interest portfolio managers also have in their own investment advisory firm or a private equity firm.

Exhibit 9.3 OPPORTUNITIES FOR PORTFOLIO MANAGERS

Motivations	N. America	S. America	Europe	Pacific Rim	Total
Hedge funds	100.0%	83.6%	64.7%	97.0%	89.0%
Mutual funds	82.7%	67.2%	52.9%	87.9%	74.8%
Investment advisory firm	53.1%	76.1%	86.3%	40.9%	61.7%
Private equity firm	42.9%	79.1%	23.5%	74.2%	55.3%

Based on a survey of 282 Portfolio managers

Hedge funds are the most attractive option as nearly nine out of ten (89.0%) portfolio managers are looking at this alternative[2]. These investment partnerships have the greatest potential for portfolio managers to be financially rewarded for their money management skills because of performance fees.[3]

Becoming a portfolio manager at a mutual fund is also attractive. When this option is pursued, the portfolio managers tend to get some sort of equity kicker as part of the enticement to move.

The third preference is to have a position at an independent investment advisory firm. When portfolio managers choose this option, they are usually compensated, in part, with an equity stake.

The final preference is to get involved in private equity deals. This usually takes the form of venture capital or merchant banking. Once again, the equity component is the draw.

Of course, these alternatives are not exclusive of each other. We know of a number of portfolio managers who have jumped ship and subsequently became involved in smaller firms where they are involved in everything from hedge funds, to mutual funds, to discretionary investment management for high-net-worth clients, to merchant banking deals. While this is a little intense, portfolio managers can get involved in more than one of the options.

Many portfolio managers are giving careful consideration to their career options. Just how many will set up their own shop or leave their current position for an equity stake in an investment fund cannot be predicted.

Going Forward

- Because of their "star status," portfolio managers are also examining their options to start or join independent advisory firms.

- They are also attracted to product-driven entrepreneurial opportunities such as hedge and mutual funds.

- Institutions are attempting to keep portfolio managers with new deferred compensation plans designed to make staying attractive.

- While portfolio managers are less likely to have the same type of client loyalty relationship managers do, their reputation for investment talent makes them formidable competitors in an independent investment advisory capacity.

[1]Investment management firms are seeing a steady rise in their portfolio managers hopping the fence for greener pastures. This trend is getting increased play by the media who report on major moves. As it is upsetting to investors, the firms are examining and experimenting with various ways to reinforce their relationships with their portfolio managers.

[2]In working with portfolio managers who want to establish their own hedge funds, we find that they are not always aware of everything that needs to go into getting a hedge fund up and running. Portfolio managers interested in setting up a hedge fund must consider the steps that need to be taken, including addressing accounting and legal issues. The prime broker must also be selected. Of great importance—the monies must be raised. While a portfolio manager's reputation can bring in some investors, what is often needed is a well developed and implemented marketing program for the hedge fund to reach its potential.

[3]With the recent changes concerning participating in hedge funds, these investment partnerships are going to increasingly look like mutual funds. Their number will be multiplying in the forthcoming years. Moreover, marketing will become a much more important function for hedge funds, especially new ones.

3

Build Your Business I: Start Right

10

Make an Informed Decision

"Homo oeconomicus is not behind us, but before us."
- Marcel Mauss

"Money is my first, last and only love."
- Armand Hammer

Whether or not to become an independent investment advisor is a hot topic for people in the industry. If you are reading this book, its probably because you, too, are interested in the possibility of "going independent" (or you recently did and are curious about other people's experiences). If you have been to any industry conferences recently, you have heard a lot of discussion in the sessions (and a whole lot more in the hallways) about independence. The issue for you should be about YOU!

We say it here, and will say it over and over again, being independent is not for everyone. Some advisors will do much better by not going independent. The decision to go independent is both a personal one and a professional one. What is critical is that you think through your options and make an informed decision.

You Should Think Through Your Options

As the last series of chapters demonstrated, there are many financial advisors who are considering going independent. Anyone who is successful as an investment advisor would be smart to think through their options. Since there are a lot of smart people in the industry, it should come as no surprise that there is a great deal of interest in independence by financial advisors (see Exhibit 10.1).

Just to recap, nearly six out of 10 brokers (59.0%) have seriously considered going out on their own, as have a majority of high-end insurance agents (57.1%). A similar proportion of accountants (60.7%) are very interested in the investment advisory business, as are a good number of relationship managers currently housed in investment management firms or banks (49.2% and 35.5% respectively). Finally, many portfolio managers (76.6%) are also considering the benefits of becoming independent investment advisors.

Exhibit 10.1 THERE IS SIGNIFICANT INTEREST IN BEING AN INDEPENDENT INVESTMENT ADVISOR

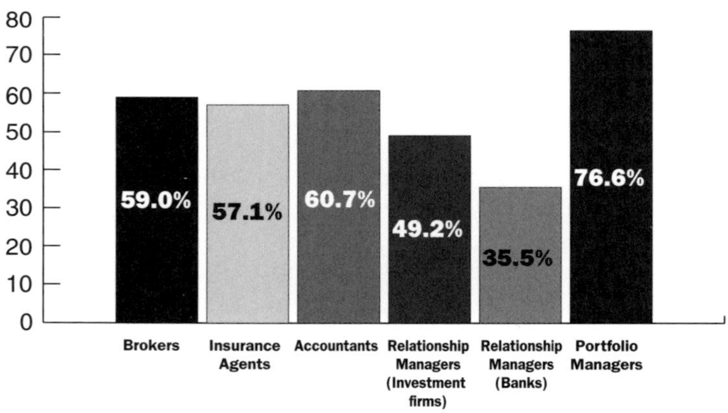

Based upon a survey of 2,225 Financial Advisors

Of course, there is a big gap between thinking and doing. While becoming an independent investment advisor is a very good choice for some people, it is a poor choice for others. Not every financial advisor should become an independent investment advisor, and not every one is going to. Being an independent investment advisor is not for everyone.

You should think through the decision carefully, and consider both sides of the coin. That is, you should look at the trade-offs in each choice. In this chapter, we will discuss what should go into your decision to go independent. But we will also look closely at staying in your current position, because there are some very good reasons for doing so. The biggest reason is that many of the financial institutions are going all out to win the loyalty of their financial advisors and their affluent clients.

Think About Staying Where You Are

This is the option most investment advisors take. They stay where they are. This might be the best choice for you, too.

The appeal of independence to some investment advisors is not lost on the financial institutions, and they are responding quickly. The financial institutions want to maintain their very successful distribution systems, and they want to keep their investment advisors happy. Financial institutions want to win the loyalty of the investment advisor in the trenches. They especially want to win over the hearts and minds of those professional advisors who are working with the affluent. They know that as career options become more plentiful, investment advisors are looking around.

Brokerage Firms

Brokerage firms are here to stay. There isn't any question about that. Brokerage firms are major players in the business of providing investment advisory services to the affluent. They are going to be major players in the investment advisory business for some time to come.

Already, brokerage firms are making the shift to fee-based businesses. In addition, they are providing their advisors with the same array of services independent advisors can obtain. For instance, many brokerage firms are establishing their own mutual fund shopping centers, through which their brokers can access much of the universe of mutual funds, including no-load funds.

Brokerage firms are rapidly adding value in the field of financial planning. They are putting programs into place that support brokers who want to provide comprehensive financial planning and a broader array of financial services to the affluent. This support takes a number of forms; they range from computerized financial plans to dedicated financial planning teams that brokers can call in.

Additional forms of value added include:

- Technical training.
- Sales and marketing training.
- Brand and product advertising.
- Turn-key prospecting and sales programs for cultivating affluent investors.

Brokerage firms are working hard, and successfully, to create loyalty among their brokers. Because of the marketing and technical muscle of the brokerage houses, staying with them may be the best choice. By comparison, being an independent investment advisor may be just too hard.

Insurance Companies

Insurance companies have confronted the issue of creating loyalty for quite some time. The insurance industry is structured so that high-end insurance agents are very likely to use the services and products of a number of different carriers. Even when they are technically career agents, high-end insurance agents tend to have contracts with multiple companies. As a result, insurance companies already understand how to work with independent producers and create loyalty.

Right now, 57.1% of high-end insurance agents are interested in being independent investment advisors. Of course, some will, but many will not.

Insurance companies are already taking action to support agents who want do more in the investment management field. Many carriers already provide producers with a wide range of products to sell. For instance, agents can obtain mutual funds and Wrap account programs through carriers. Many insurance companies are also educating agents in the concepts that underlie modern portfolio theory. Additionally, they are training agents how to find and work with affluent investors.

The goal of insurance companies is to be chosen by agents for business. Forward thinking insurance companies will continue to take steps to help their agents be effective so they, in turn, are chosen for business. A lot of producers will find this support of great value, and will decide not to go independent. This may be a good choice for you.

Private Banks and Investment Management Firms

Private banks and the larger investment management firms are in the same position as brokerage houses and insurance companies. Many relationship managers are thinking through their options and are thinking about the future.

One of the ways private banks and investment management firms are responding to the paradigm change is modifying their compensation systems. For example, some financial institutions are linking relationship manager compensation to the gathering and longevity of assets they oversee. Changes in the compensation system plus the support systems provided are motivating relationship managers to stay with private banks and investment management firms. They have rethought their options.

Think About Going Independent

Brokers, insurance agents, relationship managers and portfolio managers have to decide whether it is better to work within the structure of financial firms or go independent. Making the decision to go independent is a hard one. It is certainly not the right decision for everyone.

We will focus our discussion of thinking about going independent on brokers, insurance agents, and relationship managers. Accountants, of course, are in a different position. They already have independent practices, and are thinking of whether or not to add investment advisory companies or divisions to their firm. For them, later chapters on what is necessary to be in the business will be more useful.

There are two major sets of considerations in a decision by a broker, insurance agent or relationship manager to go independent. There are psychological considerations and there are economic considerations. If you are thinking about going off on your own, both psychological and economic considerations must be weighed.[1]

Economic considerations are fairly straightforward. You can

conduct a financial cost benefit analysis and that will tell you if a move makes bottom-line dollars and sense.

Psychological considerations are more difficult to evaluate. First we will look at the psychological considerations and then we will address the economic considerations.

Psychological Considerations

Going out on your own is being an entrepreneur. Now, brokers and insurance agents are well experienced with many of the aspects of entrepreneurship — they already have the experience of having to develop a client base and run many aspects of their business. But becoming an independent investment advisor is, for many, riskier. As an independent business person, you are working without the safety net of the brokerage firm or the carrier. Not everyone is ready for that amount of risk, or stress or pressure. Some people just don't like putting themselves in that position. Others are at a stage in life where that degree of risk is inappropriate.

So take your time thinking through your options from a psychological standpoint. Talk with family and trusted associates. Talk with your closest clients. You know how you are comfortable making big decisions. Above all, give yourself the time you need to make the right choice for you.

Here are some questions you should think about:

- Do I really want to be independent?
- Am I a true entrepreneur?
- Do I want to own my own business?
- Do I want to run my own business?
- Am I willing to give up my safety net?
- What support do I receive from the firm?
- What of my firm's services do I use?

- What value do I get for the portion of my fees I share with the firm?

- Can I effectively service my clients the way I believe they should be serviced at my firm?

When you go independent there is no safety net. There is no person such as a manager or general agent to smooth out the rough edges, to handle problems, to deal with all the paperwork.

And, there is no one but you to confront the risks. And the risks are significant. Think, for example, about what could happen if you make a bad set of initial decisions? Think about the difficulties of finding the right office space, of having to make computer hardware, software and phone system decisions, of having to recruit and train a staff and design all the personnel policies and procedures or hire someone else to do it.

Then, too, consider client risks. What will client reaction be? Will your highly satisfied clients will go with you, or back out at the last moment? Will they be prepared to move all of their assets or just a portion on a trial basis? How prepared are your clients for your move?

Then, of course, you could find you just do not like being independent. You could find you do value the supportive environment and value provided by a financial institution. The key is thinking the decision through, and that includes thinking through your options. Don't burn any bridges; make sure you keep as many options open as possible, including a possible return to your old firm.

Economic Considerations

In order to think through the economic considerations, you should get together as many numbers as possible. Good numbers and analysis will enable you to answer questions like these:

- Will there be sufficient current earnings — will revenues exceed the expenses of setting up and running the office?

- What after-tax ramifications are there?

- What possibilities for economic leverage exist?
- What kind of equity can I build in my business?

Estimating earnings is challenging. It is where many advisors make errors, because the assumptions involve the number of clients you will have, the amount of assets under management and the fee arrangement you have with each client. We find most independent investment advisors estimate their current earnings are 90% of what they take in.

Off-setting earnings are expenses. Anticipate these categories. We provide estimates, based on our research. Keep in mind that conditions change quickly in this field, and that you should not trust these numbers. Collect your own as you gather information about going independent and evaluate your options.

Expense categories include:

- Clearance — most advisors pay about 15% of what wirehouses gross; the range is from 10 - 20%.
- The cost to run the office — most advisors say it is between 15% and 30% of gross.
- Personnel — costs for people you need to help you.
- Communications — hardware, software and services (e.g. feeds for live quotes, news) and the telephone system
- Office space — whether home-based or leased office pace and improvements.
- Office equipment and supplies — copiers, mail machines, office supplies.
- Marketing materials and support.

Tax considerations are important in establishing a business. By going independent (if you are not joining a firm) you create a business entity. You will need to decide on its legal structure, whether it is to be a C corporation, a subchapter S, or limited liability company.[2] As an independent, you can create your entity to fit your financial needs and there are some tax strategies you can use. For instance, you might not be subject to the 2% limitation on expenses.

Managing equity issues are also key. When you work for a brokerage firm or an insurance company, you cannot sell your business when you want to retire. On the other hand, if you own an independent investment advisory business, you may be able to sell out later on.[3]

All of these components are part of the decision to go independent. You must carefully evaluate everyone of them in order to make a wise decision.

Re-Thinking Independence

Having thought through you decision whether or not to go independent, you are now at the point where you should re-think your options.

By re-thinking, we mean a careful consideration of your greatest asset — your existing book of business. Your greatest assets are the affluent clients with whom you have worked so very hard to establish meaningful and rewarding relationships. Their existence is what has made it possible for you to even think about the decision to go independent.

A key factor in going independent is to be able to provide your clients with an exceptional level of service. To be able to deliver great service means establishing relationships with resource warehouses. But to figure out whether you need to establish a relationship with a broker/dealer or a service firm or other resource warehouse, you need to re-think, and complete a critical evaluation of your current practice and your goals for the practice in the future.

When you are looking over resource warehouses, you have to be able to specify just what kind of support you're looking for. In effect, you must conduct a professional review of your practice.There are four components to a professional review of your practice:

- Target markets analysis.
- Financial services portfolio.

- Resource warehouse core services.
- Value-added support services.

Target Markets Analysis

A target markets analysis is the place to start. A target market analysis is an evaluation of what are now your natural markets.

Figuring out your target market is easiest if you think about your top 25 affluent clients. You should see to what extent they form a natural market.

Probably the easiest way to look at this is by source of wealth. Are your affluent clients all corporate executives? Or are they typically physicians or other professionals? Are they mostly people who inherited wealth? Or, maybe, this is not a productive way of looking at your clients.

Re-think your top 25 clients and try to observe what characteristics they have in common. Is there a group of widows? Is there a concentration of dual-career executives? Are there similarities in terms of age, sex, stage in life, profession, investment philosophy? A much more sophisticated and effective way to re-think your natural market is by using high-net-worth psychology (which we discuss in a future chapter).

The next step in re-thinking your target market evaluations is to anticipate where your affluent clients will be coming from in the future. Do you want them to be like your current natural market? Would you like to change?

For example, we know of investment advisors who have decided to target the physician market. The upside of the physician market is that with all the changes impacting the health care field, physicians have a great need for comprehensive financial planning. The down side is that all these same changes have negatively impacted physician compensation.[4] By recognizing these changes and their impact, you can decide where the opportunities lie among your target market segments.[5]

The better you understand your target markets, the more successful you will be whether you decide to go independent or not. What is so critical in understanding target markets is that you go beyond the surface by using high-net-worth psychology. The nature of your current and future target markets will basically determine what should be your optimal services portfolio.[6]

Financial Services Portfolio

The next step is for you to specify your financial services portfolio today and begin looking forward. Start by specifying what services you provide today. Think in terms of all of your financial services, not only those you provide to affluent clients. You may also consider serving the institutional market (see Appendix A).

In assessing your financial services portfolio, it is best to start by thinking in terms of the wide range of financial services that you can offer. Aside from investment advisory services, you need to consider what else you will be doing for affluent clients. Estate planning, asset protection planning and charitable giving all go beyond investment management but are sought by affluent clients. Consider retirement planning, particularly the design and administration of qualified retirement programs.[7]

In the investment advisory business itself, you need to be very clear about how you want to work in the field. You can manage money yourself. You can pick money managers. You can do a little of each. The point – the preferred resource warehouses you should employ depends on the way you provide investment advisory services. Evidently, you need to ally yourself with resource warehouses that can support your practice and the lines of business you will be promoting as well as the way you want to operate as an investment advisor.

Resource Warehouse Core Services

Your target markets influence your services portfolio and vice versa. Your financial services portfolio determines the nature of the institutional support services you will need. If you are managing the money yourself, you may require investment research, access to IPOs and prime brokerage services. On the other hand, if you are concentrating on asset gathering, you might look for the resource warehouse to conduct the asset allocation, select the securities, money managers and/or mutual funds and rebalance the portfolios.

Going beyond investment advisory services, you will need to consider your additional lines of business. If you are providing insurance, the range of companies the resource warehouse is accessing becomes very important. Together, the resource warehouse support services are the absolutely necessary services you need to be in business. Thus, you must select a resource warehouse that understands your practice and is positioned to enable you to be in business.

Value-Added Support Services

Finally, you need to determine how the resource warehouses can help you grow your practice. Independent investment advisors have some very pressing concerns about which they are seeking support. Resource warehouses are competing in terms of offering value-added services such as compliance, education, turn-key seminars and the like. Resource warehouses realize that core services will not win the loyalty of independent investment advisors, value-added services will. Your task is to identify these value-added services, and make sure you are getting the ones you need.

Thinking and Re-Thinking Your Options

Going independent is not for everyone. However, aside from setting up on your own, there are a number of options.

You can join a large or boutique broker/dealer. Before the independent broker/dealers, brokers would switch broker/dealers. Depending on the situation, some of these firms provide "front money" to attract high-end producers.

Another option is to go independent and start your own broker/dealer. This is a viable option for investment advisors with significant production (say north of $1 million). There are time and effort commitments to establish and maintain your own broker/dealer. There are also net capital requirements as well as additional operating costs such as certified financial audits.

Yet another option is to go independent by working with an independent broker/dealer or a service firm or both. The advantages can duplicate the ones you would have by starting your own broker/dealer. Furthermore, the capital requirements are not there. This option would cost you about 10% to 15% more than if you had your own broker/dealer and were using a clearing firm. However, you will probably save more than that by not having to pay expenses or to continually invest in updating technology and so forth.

Going Forward

- Going independent is not for everyone.
- You should think about staying where you are. Financial institutions are moving aggressively to make staying an attractive option.
- If you think about going independent, you should think about psychological and economic issues.
  - Psychological issues have to do with your own personality, stage in life and attitudes towards risk.
  - Economic issues are easier to quantify, but just as difficult. Costs and revenues need to be carefully projected.
- Re-thinking is the process of understanding and planning exactly what your needs will be over the next few years, including:
  - Target markets analysis
  - Financial services portfolio
  - Resource warehouse core services
  - Value-added support services

$

[1] Most independent investment advisors we work with were able to readily delineate the economic issues. However, they were not as effective at identifying all the psychological considerations. Those investment advisors who were able to do both proved to be the most satisfied with their decision to go independent. In effect, they had carefully thought and re-thought their options deciding that going independent was indeed the alternative for them.

[2] A corporate structure is critically important because of liability issues. You would also want to consider structuring your personal assets to ensure you are judgment proof.

[3] To be able to capitalize your investment advisory firm requires that the business is firm oriented as opposed to producer oriented. That is, if all the business revolved around you and you alone, there is nothing to sell. However, if the investment advisory business was a viable entity, then you can sell it.

[4] Prince, R.A., Phillips, E. K., & Apolinsky, H.I. Physician Financial Planning in a Changing Environment. CA: PMIC, 1996.

[5] ibid. For investment advisory services the greatest opportunities are in the retirement plans of physicians. Nevertheless, many physicians do have significant investable assets. By their own account, they have generally not done a very good job of growing these assets. Their more personally precarious situation coupled with this admission, is making the physician market an excellent one for astute investment advisors.

[6] This might appear straightforward, but it can all become convoluted quickly if you are dealing with complex target markets. For example, the field of settlement management is booming and it is relatively untapped. The same reasons that asset protection planning has become so popular (See Chapter 2), has made settlement management a major growth area for investment advisors who can capitalize on this trend. Working in this field requires not only investment advisory expertise, but significant insurance expertise, as well as proficiency with various trust instruments.

[7] Prince, R.A., & File, K.M. Marketing to the Affluent: A Toolkit for Life Insurance Professionals. OH: National Underwriter, 1995.

[8] 1997 Survey of Independent RIAs

11

Running Your Business

"The past and the future — far from being a matter of concern — were wholly implicit in the present."
- Henri Frankefort

"God is in the details."
- Ludwig Mies van der Rohe

Once you are running your own business, effective practice management will mean the difference between success and failure. When it is your business, you have to take care of a lot of details that your old firm once did. None of these areas will be completely new to you. As an experienced professional in your field, you already know something of planning your sales and marketing activities, managing your time and using technology. Now, however, how effective you are in each of these areas will directly affect your profitability and your success.

For this reason, we polled some of the best of the best about their way of managing their practices. In all, 192 independent investment advisors were polled on several major practice management issues:

- Practice planning.
- Time management.
- Technology.
- Compliance.
- Back office management.

Effective Practice Planning

The point of planning is to capture more assets. However, in order to reach the goal of greater effectiveness in asset capture, you need to have solid sales and marketing plans in place.

Sales Planning

Very few investment advisors know, much less plan, their sales efforts. Few know how much sales effort it takes to add assets or close an account. Few know what it costs them in sales efforts to gather assets per client.[1] When you know what sales effort is required in your practice, you can make better judgments about how to use your time. The first step in time management is sales and market planning, and sales and market planning are based on data from your practice.

You can be among the best of the best if you plan your sales efforts. You could know, for example, the average number of meetings it takes you to close a $250,000 or more discretionary investment account. If you do, you will be among the exceptional few investment advisors. In fact, 64.6% of investment advisors do not have a "precise assessment" of the number of meetings it takes to close a $250,000 or more discretionary investment account. The remaining 35.4% independent investment advisors estimate it takes them, on the average, 4.1 meetings to close a prospect.

We know that it is easier to sell current clients on additional services than it is to create new client relationships. You would think that independent investment advisors would have a clear sales plan for maintaining strong account relationships. You would think they would have a plan for the number of face to face meetings they would schedule with their affluent clients each and every year.

In fact, most do not. When asked to estimate the number of times they meet with their affluent clients annually, 66.1% independent investment advisors could not come up with a figure. We asked them to review their appointment books in order to come up with a number. Even after reviewing their appointment books and calendars, 13.5% of independent investment advisors still did not know how many times they met face-to-face with their affluent clients. Some independent investment advisors did have a number. The ones who can provide an estimate of the number of face-to-face meetings in a year with their affluent clients say it is just a little over once (1.2 times) a year.[2]

By understanding what it takes you to bring in and maintain assets under management, you are better able to determine where you should be putting in your sales efforts. If you have a mean number of meetings to close of four, is it time to cut your losses when the meetings drag out to six or seven? If you track your sales efforts you will know. Is meeting with your affluent clients once a year enough? What happens if you take, say, ten of your clients and meet with them once a quarter? Does cross selling increase? Does asset capture increase? If you carefully track sales efforts and results, you will know these answers.[3]

Planning your sales efforts in this way will allow you to begin to estimate the value of an affluent client. Certainly, the revenue they generate for you is the most direct measure. Thus, a client investing $1 million with you generates $10,000 annually. But this is only one measure of client value.

There are additional measures of client value. We think you should get used to thinking about the total value of a client. By total value of a client, we are not only talking about the revenue the affluent client generates for your firm. We are talking about potential incremental assets to be captured as well as future cross-sells. We are talking about opportunities in providing additional personal financial services as well as institutional services (see Appendix A).

Even more important than these direct revenue potentials in client value is the ability to access the affluent client's personal and professional networks.[4] The financial return due to client referrals is usually significantly greater than the direct revenues.[5]

The case for sales planning should be clear. But do not let sales planning take over your life. While you should track and plan sales efforts, your numbers do not have to be perfect. Instead, develop a conceptual understanding of these sales efforts and trade-offs. A "feel" for sales efforts, based in pretty good numbers, is all that is needed for you to make better (more profitable) decisions. [6]

A Marketing Plan

Very few independent investment advisors have a formal marketing plan.[7] We define a formal marketing plan to be: a written document where financial and strategic goals are stated, where there is a profile of the current and desired market and client base, and where there is a set of actions which will be taken to achieve the goals. There is overwhelming evidence from entrepreneurial literature, as well as our studies, that indicates that firms with a market plan are significantly more successful than firms without one.

In working with independent investment advisors, we find that the best marketing plans have the following elements:

- **Part #1:** A statement of marketing and financial goals for the short (next year) and medium (three or five years). Marketing goals include number of customers, mix (retained versus new), asset capture rates and the like.

- **Part #2:** A review of the environment in which the firm operates. Significant forces at work in the environment and a review of significant competition.

- **Part #3:** A set of marketing programs designed to meet the marketing and financial goals. These could include such elements as setting new sales targets (e.g., three meetings a year with current clients), or prospecting programs (e.g., four seminars, a direct mail program).

- **Part #4:** A resource program. The resource requirements you need to attain these goals (financial and professional) need to be explained. For example, you may look at the sales demands of the prospecting and retention programs and find you simply do not have the time without outsourcing some aspect of practice management.

- **Part #5:** A tracking program. The most effective entrepreneurs and business managers have boiled their program down to a few parameters that they watch very closely. To know how effective your marketing program is you need to know where you have been, where you are going, and how you are doing right now.

With a marketing and a sales plan in place, you are prepared to implement an asset capture strategy.

Using Sales Planning and Marketing Planning to Implement an Asset Capture Strategy for Selected Clients

The wealthier the client, the less likely you have all of their investable assets. If you are like most investment advisors, you promote the idea of investment portfolio diversification. Well, affluent investors do diversify their portfolio. They also almost always diversify by using a number of investment advisors.[8]

One of your objectives should be to gain a larger "share of wallet." The way to capture more assets is with a comprehensive asset capture strategy built on your sales plan and your marketing plan. An asset capture strategy has three phases:

- **Phase I:** High-impact relationship management. For the most part, only highly satisfied affluent clients will give you more assets to manage. Therefore, it is essential to employ the I-CLAS model in order to acquire more assets to invest.

- **Phase II:** Ascertain asset transfer opportunities. Evaluate your affluent clients and identify those who will be able to provide you with more assets.[9] Investment advisors who have been very successful at this have formalized this phase. They have made this a central part of their marketing plans.

- **Phase III:** Solicit additional assets. It is essential to ask for the assets to manage. Of course, you must adapt the approach to each affluent client. The 7 step approach to asking for referrals can be modified for this purpose.

If you are like many independent investment advisors, you agree on the need, in principle, for sales, marketing and asset capture planning, but feel constantly out of time. That is why effective time management is a critical piece of effective practice management.

Effective Time Management

Are you too wrapped up in administrative details? Are you stressed out because you are not being as attentive to your better affluent clients as you would like? Are you spending your time most effectively?

If you are like the majority of independent investment advisors, the answers are: yes, yes and no. Most investment advisors are not doing a very good job of managing their time. They often are more involved in putting out fires than in firing up their business. In fact, dealing with administrative matters ranks as the number one activity for the 192 independent investment advisors surveyed. But they do not like it. When we asked how important administrative matters should be, investment advisors would put it dead last (see Exhibit 11.1).

Where independent investment managers want to spend their time is in relationship management. Independent investment advisors know that a critical determinant of success in working with independent clients is how many times you are in contact with them over a period of time.[10] But even though investment advisors want to spend most of their time working with their affluent clients, relationship management ranks fourth in terms of actual time spent.

After taking care of current clients, independent investment advisors would most like to prospect and sell new clients. Ideally, prospecting and selling would be ranked second. In fact, it is ranked third.

Portfolio management was ranked second and would ideally be number third. That is, independent investment managers would rather prospect and sell than manage portfolios, and find they have to manage portfolio instead of prospecting and selling.

Independent investment advisors would like to do more professional development. Professional development is ranked fifth and advisors would rather it be number four.

Clearly, independent investment advisors understand the need for the client-facing activities of relationship management and prospecting and selling. They know they should be spending their time on marketing — prospecting, selling and relationship management. However, they are too involved in day-to-day administrative matters to spend their time building their practice.

Exhibit 11.1 ACTUAL AND IDEAL USE OF TIME

Activities	Actual Rank	Ideal Rank
Administrative matters	1	5
Portfolio management	2	3
Prospecting and selling	3	2
Relationship management	4	1
Professional development	5	4

192 Independent investment advisors interviewed

We have found that independent investment advisors will more efficiently manage their time when they clearly understand how they are spending their time. While they know where their time goes, by really keeping track, they automatically make changes for the better. An analysis of your appointment book will give you a good rough cut on where you are spending most of your time.

With that in hand, go ahead and actually track your activities for a few weeks. This simple technique is almost always very revealing. Advisors tell us they never really knew before just how efficient or inefficient they were. Time tracking takes all the guesswork out of how you are spending your time on a day-to-day basis. Once you know how you are spending your time, you can make better use of your time.[11]

Effective Use of Technology

The most important uses of technology in the private wealth industry are:

- Support the management of the client relationship.
- Portfolio management.
- Transaction processing and reporting.[12]

Back-office systems are critical to independent investment advisors. All independent investment advisors (100.0%) believe back-office transaction systems are critically important (see Exhibit 11.2). Efficient and effective back-offices are what makes independent investment advisors the number one competitor for affluent clients.

What do independent investment advisors want in their back-office transaction systems? There are a number of features that are essential, including:

- Daily account data.
- Multiple views of account data (e.g., the ability to group accounts).
- Complete integration with portfolio software and client services software (e.g., positions, balances, transaction details, account/registration information, etc.).
- The ability to easily transfer data from the portfolio management and accounting software into the custodial software (e.g., export account groups, orders, account labels, etc.).

About nine out of ten investment advisors (88.0%) say portfolio accounting and reporting software is extremely important. Slightly fewer (85.4%) think that client services and database software is extremely important. Independent investment advisors need to have everything about their clients at their fingertips. This software should enable the advisor to define fields so that they can customize it to their unique situation.

Sales presentation software is of great importance to 74.9% of independent investment advisors. Employing software to more effectively close business is increasingly attractive to investment advisors. The best know that some clients really value the extra effort, and are experienced enough to know that other clients like it kept very simple.

Portfolio management software is extremely important to 61.1% of independent investment advisors. Not all investment advisors construct investment portfolios, so this software only appeals to those who do. For those interested in this software, the trend is toward comprehensive asset allocation and portfolio modeling (that is, the ability to understand the true underlying asset allocation across a number of mutual funds).

Exhibit 11.2 THE MOST IMPORTANT TECHNOLOGY

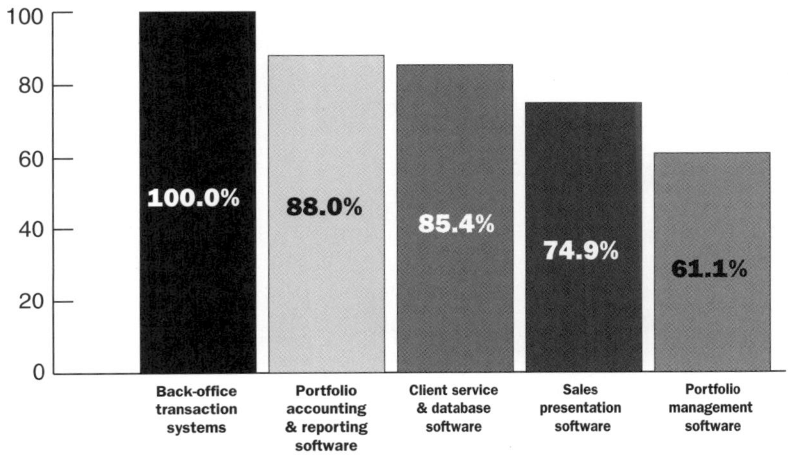

Base upon information from 192 Independent investment advisors

What independent investment advisors are looking for is seamless, hands-free software. They want a truly integrated technology solution. They want the custodial system integrated with all the software, the portfolio management and client servicing systems. Without question, this is the future of technology.

As we have seen, technology has enabled independent investment advisors to be independent. As a result, the majority of advisors see their own use of technology as a means of making the sales process even more effective. They also want technology to help them do a better job managing affluent client relationships.

There are a number of financial institutions ready and able to provide you with the back office support systems you need. Collectively, they are known as resource warehouses. Resource warehouses include investment management firms and mutual fund companies that are leveraging their expertise in administrative systems for investment management to the independent sector.

If you do decide to build an independent investment advisory business, you may very well end up doing business with one or more of these financial firms. When it comes to back-office systems, there are two types of resource warehouses that you will need to consider as they provide different sorts of services. These are independent broker/dealers and services firms.

There are quite a number of independent broker/dealers who are interested in talking to you about the services they provide. All of the independent broker/dealers are looking to expand their network of advisors. In addition, there are also a number of excellent service firms eager to help independent investment advisors.

Outsourcing the Back Office

You want to focus on the human and investment management sides of your business. You want to focus on front office issues of handling clients and their investment objectives. You will be able to concentrate on the front office if you do a good job outsourcing the back office.

Whether you place your back office with a broker/dealer or a service firm or a combination of both, you will need to consider a number of factors in order to make a well informed decision. No "back office" is perfect in all respects; there are trade-offs to be made. There are a number of factors you'll need to consider, including:

The financial strength of the back office. You need the back office to be there for you in the future. You need a back office with the financial resources to insure they stay at the forefront of technology. For instance, if you are considering using an independent broker/dealer, you should obtain financial data on the broker/dealers you are considering. If they are a public company, this is easy. If not, you can still acquire the broker/dealer's Focus Report. You can also get the broker/dealer's Annual Financial Report, Form X-17A-5.

Technology. The quality of the systems are what the back office is all about. The functionality of the back office must meet your needs. Thus, you need to ensure that the systems are state-of-the-art and that they can perform as you need them to. For example, the back offices of different service companies have somewhat different functionality. You need to carefully evaluate what they offer against what you need.

Compliance considerations. In the heavily regulated financial services industry, you need your back office to be current on compliance issues. Meet the personnel at the back office responsible for compliance, discuss programs dealing with compliance and explore how to obtain Errors and Omission insurance.

Expenses. Costs and expenses are easy to compare among back offices. With broker/dealers, for instance, evaluate payout schedules. With service companies, assess fees schedules. With both, look closely at how you have to trade-off expense costs for services.

Commitment to your business. The world of the independent investment advisor is fairly new. There are not any professionals among the back offices with that many years of experience working with independent investment advisors. While they will most likely have extensive experience in related areas, you should look for officers of the back office who have a very good understanding of the world of the independent investment advisor. They must recognize what you need to do to be successful, and be committed to help you achieve this success. You are looking for a business relationship with people willing to take steps to help you build your business.

You need to be very careful when selecting a firm to provide back-office services. Switching firms is a difficult process, so you want to choose well. Take your time and get all the information and input you can. Here are some of the ways to be careful:

- Evaluate all recruiting literature available from the firm.

- Visit the home office as well as local satellite offices (if applicable).

- Interview current investment advisors who are clients of the firm for their experiences.

- Speak with the people who will be responsible for you. This includes the traders, relationship managers and so forth.

- Look for indications that they understand your world. Also, see if the back office is more than just a back office. That is, are they involved in offering the value added services that will help you be more successful.

- Carefully review the contracts. It is a good idea to have your attorney look them over as well.

Transferring Your Book of Business

Whether you move your book to an independent broker/dealer or to a service company, the process is similar. For simplicity's sake we will briefly review how to move your book to a broker/dealer. Moving to a service company involves the same steps.

When you move to an independent broker/dealer, you will have to move both your securities license as well as your accounts. There are two ways to transfer your securities license.

Filing a U-4 Form with the Center Registration Department of the NASD. This will usually take from 7 to 10 days.

Employ the Temporary Agent Transfer system. Not all broker/dealers use this system. However, if your new broker/dealer does use the system and you're eligible, the transfer can occur the same day you make the request.[13] The Temporary Agent Transfer system is not available in California or Washington D.C.

You can usually transfer your client accounts by employing the Automatic Customer Account Transfer System. Most independent broker/dealers utilize the system. There are four steps to using the system:

- **Step #1.** You establish a new account for each client with the new broker/dealer. This includes having each client sign a form giving the old broker/dealer instructions on moving the account.

- **Step #2.** The new broker/dealer processes the forms.

- **Step #3.** The old broker/dealer is notified of the client's request, validates the instructions and then provides transfer instructions to the new broker/dealer.

- **Step #4.** The old broker/dealer transfers the securities to the new broker/dealer.

By using the Automatic Customer Account Transfer System, you can usually transfer your book of business within two weeks (assuming, of course, that all the paper work is completed properly). Some types of securities will not transfer through the Automatic Customer Account Transfer System. These include life insurance policies, annuities and some partnerships. You will have to transfer these to your new broker/dealer outside the Automatic Customer Account Transfer System.

Whether you use an independent broker/dealer or a service company, keep in mind that these firms have worked with many other advisors in the past. They have experienced staff which will make the transition as painless as possible. They will walk you through the entire transfer process.

Compliance Issues

When you are an independent investment advisor, you are responsible for complying with all securities laws and regulations. This means you need to be up to date on all the changes in laws and regulations and in compliance with them. Compliance also involves making sure all required forms are filed and current.

For smaller independent investment advisory firms as well as advisors seeking to become registered, compliance is a difficult process. Compliance audits are possible. If compliance is not handled right, it can open you up to negative consequences. That is why you should use outside experts when it comes to compliance.[14]

Because compliance is complex and because of the exposure and liability involved, some individuals decide not to go independent.

Going Forward

- Effective practice management means getting on top of several interrelated issues:
  - Practice planning

  - Time management
  - Technology
  - Compliance

- Effective practice planning involves sales planning (allocating your time among various sales activities) and marketing planning (creating and implementing a strategic development plan). Sales and market planning converge in implementing an asset capture strategy.

- Time management is the day to day discipline that enables you to act on your sales, marketing and asset capture plans. Independent investment advisors are finding that a trap is spending too much time on unproductive activities and not enough time on productive ones.

- Effective management of technology, especially for back office systems, is essential in practice management. Increasingly, the field is technology driven, and successful independent advisors are the ones forcing themselves to become expert in technology.

- Compliance issues usually require outside support.

$

[1] 1997 Survey of Independent RIAs

[2] The investment advisors tended to meet with their affluent clients annually to review their portfolios. As we will see later this is not the way to build meaningful relationships with your clients. Instead, the objective is to meet and meet often, focusing on gaining a greater understanding and devising ways to meet client needs.

[3] Part of the tracking should take into account the wealthy people you are dealing with. We have found that there will be significant variation among the different affluent investor personalities when it comes to creating baselines concerning asset gathering and maintenance. Therefore, as you refine your tracking data, you will need to employ high-net-worth psychology.

[4] Recognize that each highly satisfied affluent client should result in at least one referral that becomes a new client every two years. See: Prince R.A. & File K.M., Cultivating the Affluent: How to Segment and Service the High-Net-Worth Market. N.Y.: Institutional Investor, 1995.

[5] Over the last two years, we have been extensively studying and quantifying the total value of affluent clients. These analyses have shown that different affluent investor personalities will probably produce different total client values. With this information in hand, it is possible for an investment advisor to calculate (at the 0.5 confidence level) an affluent investor's total value over the lifetime of the relationship.

[6] The situation will determine the degree of precision. There may be times when exact calculations are required. While computing exact figures might appear daunting, spreadsheets and algorithms have been developed that makes the task quite manageable.

[7] 1997 Survey of Independent RIAs

[8] Prince R.A. & File K.M., Cultivating the Affluent: How to Segment and Service the High-net-worth Market. N.Y.: Institutional Investor, 1995.

[9] By providing estate planning services — including variations such as charitable estate planning and asset protection planning — investment advisors can effectively position themselves to determine where additional pools of assets are and help in accessing them. Additionally, you can move from providing institutional investment advisory services if you are providing individual investment advisory services and vice versa.

[10] Prince, R.A., and File, K.M. Cultivating the Affluent II: Leveraging High-Net-Worth Client and Advisor Relationships. N.Y.: Institutional Investor, 1997.

[11] There are numerous time management systems that you can use to husband your time and focus your efforts. However, to achieve optimal results requires that you adopt these systems to the investment advisory business. To date, none of the systems are geared to the investment advisory business. However, by drawing on existing systems coupled with the research, investment advisors can be shown how to optimize their time.

[12] Maude, D. & Molyneux, P. Private Banking: Maximizing Performance in a Competitive Market. London: Euromoney Publications, 1996.

[13] Eligibility requires that you live in the United States, that you have formally terminated your relationship with your former broker/dealer, that there is not any pending disciplinary or compliance problems and that you have current registration forms on file with the NASD.

[14] One of the top firms in this area is National Regulatory Services, Inc. located at 323-A Main Street, Lakeville, CT.

4

Build Your Business II: Leveraging Professional Relationships

12

Build Supportive Resource Warehouse Relationships

"There is something much more scarce, something finer far, something rarer than ability. It is the ability to recognize ability."
- Elbert Hubbard

"To succeed is to anticipate the future with a strategy."
- Armand Hammer

Resource warehouses are the supporting systems that allow investment advisors to be independent. Resource warehouses provide proprietary products, back-office systems, and value-added services.

Who Wants to do Business with Independent Investment Advisors?

The short answer is everyone. As we have seen, independent investment advisors are already an important conduit to the affluent market. And, the share of the affluent market handled by independent investment advisors is increasing. All of the companies creating financial products and services are eager to distribute them through independent advisors. Financial institutions which used to provide their products and services exclusively to their own clients are now scrambling to provide them more widely through the new independent advisor channel. Those moving to position themselves as resource warehouses include independent broker/dealers, service firms, brokerage firms, mutual fund companies, money management firms, insurance companies and private banks and trust companies.

Resource warehouses offer one, two or three types of support to independent investment advisors:

- Products.
- Back office systems.
- Value-added services.

One category of support is products.[1] Independent investment advisors need to be able to bring a wide array of product solutions to their clients' needs, and financial institutions which formerly distributed product exclusively to their private clients are now positioning themselves to sell more widely.

A second category of support is the back office systems, essential in the investment management world. For some companies, providing back office support is their core business; others offer it as an adjunct to their products.

The third category of resource warehouse support is value-added-services. We have provided an overview of the various types of resource warehouses in Exhibit 12.1.

Although you can use this analysis as a general map of who is providing resource warehouse support, keep in mind that this is a fast moving field, and things change quickly. Before selecting the few institutions you will rely on as your resource warehouses, you should network extensively and gather a lot of data. Keep in mind that product lines and back office systems support are rapidly becoming commodities; they are quite similar regardless of who is providing them. Keep your eye out for the value-added services that are really what differentiate resource warehouses today.

Let's review the various types of resource warehouses extremely interested in working with independent investment advisors.

Independent Broker/Dealers

There are many independent broker/dealers looking to hold security licenses and handle transactions for independent investment advisors. In an earlier chapter, we discussed how to go about selecting a broker/dealer. A large part of this decision

Exhibit 12.1 COMPARING THE RESOURCE WAREHOUSES

Resource Warehouses	Proprietary Products	Back-Office Systems	Value-added Services
Independent Brokers/Dealers	This is rarely the case	This is their core business	High priority – in order to differentiate themselves
Service Firms	No	This is their core business	High priority – in order to differentiate themselves
Brokerage Firms	Yes, but currently using nonproprietary products as well	Provided through "separate units"	Have not recognized the need
Mutual Fund Companies	This is their core business	Provided through "separate units" to particular providers	Increased development of such services
Money Management Firms providing cutomized Individual Investment Portfolios	This is their core business	No	Increased development of such services
Insurance Companies	This is their core business	Provided through "separate units"	Increased development of such services
Private Banks and Trust Companies	This is their core business	Save for trust services–this tends not to be the focus	Very limited to date

should be based on your self-assessment and an analysis of the lines of business you will engage in.

However, broker/dealers are rapidly piling on value-added services to attract new, independent investment advisors. They are rapidly expanding beyond basic transaction processing and are providing a range of additional services to try and win the business of more independent investment advisors. Such value-added services can include support in mutual fund selection, assisting in moving from commission based to fee-based compensation, prospecting support, and dealing with compliance concerns. These can be vital to your practice, so seek out the broker/dealers providing these services and evaluate them carefully.

Service Firms

For fee-based investment advisors, the need for back-office technology is essential. Service firms, including custodial companies and clearing firms, provide a variety of technical support services such as consolidated accounting. Some service firms can also provide a variety of administrative services for trusts as well as retirement plans.

Service firms are also looking to get a larger share of the independent investment advisor market by providing state-of-the-art technology coupled with a variety of value-added services. Some work in conjunction with independent broker/dealers and some compete.

Brokerage Firms

As you know, traditional brokerage firms are not standing still. Some are staking out a new middle ground between the traditional brokerage firm/broker arrangement and the independent broker/dealer and independent investment advisor arrangement. What they are doing is entering into new types of contracts with brokers. Under these contracts, they allow brokers to have a higher payout on their production but make them responsible for more of the costs.[2]

Larger brokerage companies are using the clearing firms they own to provide services to independent investment advisors.[3] Although this can create channel conflict with the brokerage firms' own house brokers, it indicates how fluid the situation has become.[4]

Mutual Fund Companies

Independent advisors are becoming a very important channel of distribution for mutual funds. As a result, fund companies are very interested in winning the loyalty of independent investment advisors, and the fund companies are aggressively putting programs in place to win loyalty.

To date, no mutual fund company has yet been able to establish itself as the dominant player among independent investment advisors. Save for some index fund families, no mutual fund company has more than a 4% share of assets under management by independent investment advisors.[5] For the foreseeable future, mutual fund companies will continue to aggressively compete for your business and that of other independent investment advisors.[6]

Money Management Firms Providing Customized Individual Investment Portfolios

Like the mutual fund companies, money management firms are also looking for ways of getting their products to the affluent market. They provide their services directly through intermediaries and through Wrap account programs.

These money management firms are in the same position as the mutual fund companies. The market is highly fragmented and they are eager to increase their share. Since they typically have a "small share of portfolio" of any single independent investment advisor,[7] they welcome advisors who are able to bring assets with them.

Insurance Companies

The brokering of insurance products is a well established line of business. As the independent investment advisor distribution system has grown, insurance companies have responded with more resources.

Traditionally, the insurance companies have focused their efforts on independent broker/dealers. Thus, by building strong relationships with these independent broker/dealers, insurance companies have had access to independent investment advisors. Now, in addition to the independent broker/dealers, many insurance companies are developing programs directly for the independent investment advisor.[8]

Private Banks and Trust Companies

Because of the leverage created by working through independent investment advisors, a number of private banks and trust companies are seeking to extend their reach by also using this distribution system to market their services.[9] Aside from investment advisory and back-office technology, private banks and trust companies are also offering such services as credit, transaction services and a broad range of fiduciary services.

How Resource Warehouses Add Value

We suggest a two step process for evaluating your resource warehouse options. You should first sort resource warehouses into categories based on the quality of their products and back office services. Although these are rapidly becoming commodities (a sector fund is a sector fund, etc.), they still vary in quality in the way all credence services do.

Once you have narrowed your choice down to several with the right level of quality, you should look hardest at the value-added services. Resource warehouses are recognizing that in order to win the long-term loyalty of independent investment advisors, they need to add value.

This idea parallels the way you have to work with your affluent investor clients. It's not enough to construct an investment portfolio for them, there are any number of advisors who can do that. You have to add value in some personal way. As we have discussed, adding value can mean different things in different situations with people in different market segments. But while the ways to add value may be different, the need to add value is always there.

The same is true for the resource warehouses. They need to add value in order to attract you and other independent investment advisors. But they each add value in different, personal ways. This means that you can significantly affect what adding value means. You and your fellow independent investment advisors can influence the quality and type of support services provided by the resource warehouses whose services and products you use. Let's look at a few examples of value-added support. These examples were selected because they are needed by many independent investment advisors and because they are now being provided by some of the resource warehouses.

Educational Programs

Like you, independent investment advisors are hungry for any information that can make them more effective in their practices. Providing information is what educational programs do best, and educational programs are one way to make independent investment advisors more effective. There are a number of ways resource warehouses provide education to independent investment advisors.

One way education is commonly provided is through conferences. An advantage of conferences is that advisors have the opportunity to choose which sessions are of particular interest to them. Many independent investment advisors report that they get a great deal out of educational conferences. There are also disadvantages to conferences, however. Most advisors we poll say that attending meetings does not always translate into building their practices or dealing with important concerns.[10]

To fill this gap, another type of educational program that some resource warehouses are providing are workshops. In effect, the resource warehouses are creating learning environments for the users of their products and services. With the intimacy, convenience and focus that small groups provide, workshops offer significant advantages in the minds of financial professionals.[11] The cost of workshops are usually split between the resource warehouse and the participants.

Moving up the cost and intensity ladder are coaching programs. The effectiveness of well designed and managed coaching programs has been demonstrated among high-end insurance agents.[12] These programs have been able to take very successful insurance agents and help them reach an even higher level of professional and personal development. The success of coaching programs depends on how marketing and practice development issues are handles. Coaching programs are more costly for both resource warehouses and independent investment advisors. Resource warehouses commonly divide the costs with participants.

These programs generally benefit everyone involved. Because of value-added educational programs, independent investment advisors are more productive. In return, participating advisors are happy to do business, often increased business, with the resource warehouse.

Of course, educational programs are only as good as the quality of the programs as well as the quality of those responsible for the program. You will be able to quickly discriminate between the people who do it well and those who do it less well. We have empirically found three factors to be key; content expertise, facility with applying adult learning principles,[13] and content which is right on target.

Marketing Support

Marketing support is an important area of value-added services. Marketing support is in consistent high demand among independent investment advisors. Until recently, our studies showed that independent investment advisors were too dependent on relatively indirect marketing strategies. Even worse, we have found that less than 10% of independent investment advisors have formal marketing plans. Independent investment advisors are becoming more aggressive about marketing their services. As a group, independent investment advisors will double their direct expense annual marketing budget over the next five years.[14]

The big area in marketing support programs is prospecting support. Prospecting support is in great demand from independent investment advisors.[15] Investment advisors are particularly interested in professional advisor (e.g., attorney) referral programs and turn-key prospecting seminars.

Other results-oriented marketing and sales training is demanded by independent investment advisors. There is much interest in training in how to develop key markets such as the affluent, family business owners or physicians. Successful marketing of products such as the 401(k) business are also of considerable interest to independent investment advisors.[16] Independent investment advisors require that the training be highly specific, generic training is usually viewed as useless by these experienced professionals.

Another big area in training is in relationship marketing and client retention. How to create very strong relationships with clients is of tremendous importance to independent investment advisors. The experience of the best investment advisors confirms our research findings. It is possible to build relationships of such strength that even when investment portfolios drop in value, clients will continue to invest and refer. Like all skills, relationship management can be taught and learned, and investment advisors are interested in making sure that their skills are state-of-the-art.

Wholesaler Talent

Another value-added benefit of working with resource warehouses is access to the skills and expertise of their wholesalers.[17] Right now, wholesalers are an underutilized talent. Pioneering independent investment advisors have begun to leverage wholesaler talent by forming advisory boards or resource groups of wholesalers. There are a number of ways to benefit from the abilities and strengths of wholesalers:[18]

- Wholesalers who are excellent at public speaking for seminars. Seminars are one of the best ways to generate new business. High-quality seminars are very effective in motivating affluent individuals to become clients. Wholesalers who can help you build your business by putting on high-quality seminars with you are major assets that will make you more successful

- Wholesalers who are great in one-to-one situations. The ability to meet an affluent investor and convert them to a client is a very valuable skill. A wholesaler that can close business with you will help you grow your practice. Related to this is the wholesaler who can get you in the door, a rarer talent.

- Wholesalers who generate good sales ideas. Wholesalers deal with lots of investment advisors. They have a great perspective on which sales ideas work and which ones do not. A wholesaler who provides you with new perspectives on ways to get and close business is invaluable.

- Wholesalers who are excellent mentors. Helping investment advisors be more effective is what the best wholesalers are all about. The optimal situation is a wholesaler who has the expertise to assist you in growing your business by helping you with creating a highly efficient and effective practice.

Of course, in order to enlist a wholesaler to work on your behalf you will need to establish a two-way partnership. In exchange for the efforts of the wholesalers you work closest with, you will need to use their services and/or products. Our research shows that wholesalers have a significant impact on advisors' product and service decisions.[19]

Converting to a Fee-Based Investment Advisory Business.

Another major concern of independent investment advisors is converting from a commission based business to a fee-based business.[20] Most investment advisors recognize that they have to make this transition. However, many do not know how to make the transition efficiently.

This has provided the resource warehouse (especially the independent broker/dealers) with another way of adding value. Some of them have developed compensation transition programs. They will work with independent investment advisors and provide a process and support system for making the transition. Keep in mind that an effective compensation transition will take a number of years.[21]

Compliance Considerations

It's not only marketing support that resource warehouses are providing to independent investment advisors. There are other areas such as compliance issues that are of considerable concern to independent investment advisors.[22] Compliance issues are important because regulations change often and adherence is critical to maintaining an investment business.

Selecting Resource Warehouses to Partner With

Today, financial institutions are both competing for the same clients as well as cooperating by working together. "Co-optition" is the term used to describe this phenomena of competing and cooperating simultaneously.[23] The largest financial institutions use each other's services (such as brokerage) while they go after the same markets.

Independent investment advisors are also engaged in co-optition. Independent investment advisors cooperate with financial institutions by obtaining products and services from them in their function as resource warehouses. Investment advisors compete with financial institutions by targeting the same affluent investors.[24] Another example of co-optition is when a money manager with a private client group may also have some mutual funds that would benefit your affluent clients. Yet another example of co-optition is when independent investment advisors create support networks. In networks, they share information with potential direct competitors.

There is a significant difference in the relationship possibilities when you look at a resource warehouse as a vendor and when you look at a resource warehouse as a partner (see Exhibit 12.2). When you think of resource warehouses as vendors, you concentrate on maximizing the value to you of every single transaction, and limit your exchange to direct products and services. For their part, the resource warehouse will see you as just one of many advisors and they will have a limited understanding of your business and goals.

On the other hand, if you think of your relationship with a resource warehouse as a partnership (or strategic alliance) interactions are relationship oriented. This means you are as aware of benefits to the resource warehouse as to yourself and your business. You rely on the resource warehouse for a variety of value-added services, such as the ones we talked about in this chapter. In return, the resource warehouse demonstrates a concern about the current and future success of your business, and is able to support your goals because of their deep understanding of your firm.

Exhibit 12.2 RESOURCE WAREHOUSES AS VENDORS VERSUS PARTNERS

As a Vendor	As a Partner
Transaction oriented	Relationship oriented
Independent investment advisors are seen as readily replaceable	Sincere concern about the well-being of their independent investment advisors
Limited understanding of your business	Extensive understanding of your business
Only provides investment products and services	Provides investment products and services, as well as value-added services that help you grow your business

In order to migrate your relationships with resource warehouses from one of a vendor to a partnership, you should think through several steps.

Step #1: Evaluate Your Resource Warehouse Relationships

The first thing to do is to evaluate all the resource warehouse relationships you have. How satisfied are you with them?

What value-added services do they provide? How committed and supportive do they seem?

Step #2: Learn About Your Options

You should also ask around, using your network of other independent investment advisors, and find out what their experience has been. Look for two things — what are the value-added services being offered which you may be interested in, and what firms seem to be doing the best job of partnering with independent advisors. You may uncover another resource warehouse to try.

As you work through this process, keep talking to the resource warehouse people. Ask them how they think about the relationship, and what support they could provide. Test new ideas out on them. You will be able to tell by their responsiveness how interested they are in partnering with you.

Step #3: Make an Informed Decision

Once you have done your homework, gathered a lot of information and tested out new ways of thinking about the relationship with your resource warehouses, you will be able to settle on the one or two which give you the most advantages. Then, like working with your affluent clients, you invest time and energy into making the relationship work well for both parties. Of course, just like working with your wealthy clients, keep your eye out for new opportunities.

Going Forward

- Resource warehouses offer three types of services to independent investment advisors:
  - Investment products.
  - Back office services.
  - Value-added services.
- The first two are rapidly becoming commodities. You should evaluate product and back office systems quality and value closely

- Resource warehouses are differentiating themselves on the basis of value-added services. Value-added services include:
  - Educational programs.
  - Marketing support.
  - Wholesaler talent.
  - Converting to a fee-based investment advisory business.
  - Compliance considerations.
- You can use resource warehouses as vendors or create partnership relationships with them Partnership relationships create significant leverage for your firm
- There are three steps to creating partnerships with resource warehouses:
  - **Step #1:** Evaluate Your Resource Warehouse Relationships.
  - **Step #2:** Learn About Your Options.
  - **Step #3:** Make an Informed Decision.

$

[1] We are using a very broad definition of products. We are not only talking about investments such as mutual funds and individual securities, we are also talking about things like investment research.

[2] Regional brokerage firms have taken the lead in this "way of doing business." To be competitive, and effectively attract quality brokers, these regionals are creating semi-independent broker networks. Some of the senior managers of independent broker/dealers expect this trend to continue. They predict that the warehouses will also start some sort of program creating a semi-independent environment for selected brokers.

[3] In this respect, the brokerage firms are competing directly with the services firms.

[4] Based on a series of competitive assessments, from an institutional perspective, brokerage firms would significantly benefit from providing selected services to independent investment advisors. Advantages would not only come from a greater utilization of back-office systems, but would also come from another distribution systems for investment products. However, for the brokerage firm to obtain the latter benefit requires the development of a lock-step services migration strategy.

[5] 1997 Survey of Independent RIAs

[6] 1997 Survey of Independent RIAs

[7] Preliminary research shows extensive parallels to the findings of the 1997 Survey of Independent RIAs

[8] Prince, R.A. "Independent Investment Advisors: An Alternative Distribution System for Insurance Companies." Probe, in press.

[9] Presently, while numerous private banks and trust companies are "evaluating" independent investment advisors as a distribution system, few have attempted to develop a presence among them. A large part of the problem is a clash of cultures. The entrepreneurial orientation of independent investment advisors causes problems for many financial institutions, especially private banks and trust companies. Nevertheless, a handful of private banks and trust companies have made considerable inroads among independent investment advisors. Their growing success is predicated on a broad understanding of the world of the independent investment advisor coupled with a structure that mirrors their own.

[10] Based on extensive analyses of the ratings sheets from all types of financial professionals, including independent investment advisors who have attended educational conferences, find that they see the time they invested as worthwhile. However, in follow-up interviews, few implement the ideas and concepts. Still, the overwhelming majority would eagerly attend similar events. Their interest in attending educational conferences is a function of the content coupled with the quality of the presenters. For independent investment advisors, the content must center on their key concerns; See 1997 Survey of Independent RIAs

[11] Prince, R.A. "Study Finds 'Road Shows' Work Best for Top Agents." National Underwriter, 100 (29), 1996.

[12] Prince, R.A. "'Coaching' Fills in Gaps for Experienced Agents." National Underwriter, 100 (34), 1996.

[13] For a discussion of some key adult leaning principles see: Schwatz, R.M. The Skilled Facilitator: Practical Wisdom for Developing Effective Groups. San Francisco: Jossey-Bass, 1994.

[14] 1997 Survey of Independent RIAs

[15] 1997 Survey of Independent RIAs, Also see: Prince, R.A. "High-end Agents Seek More Prospecting Support." National Underwriter, 100 (26), 1996.

[16] 1997 Survey of Independent RIAs

[17] The term wholesalers is generic. Different firms employ different terms such as "account executives," "relationship managers" and "business development specialists." In the final analysis, the responsibility of these people is to work with investment advisors to help them grow their business. In exchange for the support, the wholesalers hope that the investment advisors will use the services and/or products of their firm. Thus, at their core, irrespective of the title used, all these professionals are wholesalers.

[18] Murry, N. The Excellent Investment Advisor. NY: Nicholas Murry, 1996.

[19] 1997 Survey of Independent RIAs

[20] ibid.

[21] There are empirically validated migration strategies for moving from a predominantly commission based practice to a principally fee-based and even fee-only practice. This transition can be slightly painful in the short-run but is more professionally rewarding over time. It's important to map out the transition taking advantage of the good and bad experiences of those that have already migrated. Otherwise, it is very likely you will repeat their mistakes and fail to do all the "right things."

[22] 1997 Survey of Independent RIAs

[23] Brandenbuger, A.M., and Nalebuff, B.J. Co-optition. N.Y.: Doubleday, 1996.

[24] In some independent investment advisor circles, these is a lot of concern over competition from resource warehouses. While anyone would prefer less competition, it is inevitable that everyone will end up, at some level, competing with each other. Moreover, it is highly unlikely that the more diversified resource warehouses will not make efforts to cultivate the affluent. The wealthy are just too attractive a market (see Chapter 1). What is really important for independent investment advisors is that the resource warehouse they use, provide them with what they need, including extensive value-added services. Finally, as this is a relationship based business, rarely, can a monolithic financial institution compete against a high-end independent investment advisor and win.

13

Is an Advisor Network for You?

"There ain't no rules around here! We're trying to accomplish something!"
- Thomas Edison

"The idea that life is essentially based on intellect, and that intellect is accepted in practical life as the most valuable of our mental energies, goes hand in hand with the growth of the money economy."
- Georg Simmel

It seems as if every newsletter or magazine you pick up these days is doing a feature on advisor networks and study groups. The Alpha Group is a typical advisor network. The Alpha Group is a network of nine independent investment advisors. They created the Alpha Group because they felt they could be more effective sharing information.

Advisor networks and study groups are growing in popularity. There are now more study groups and networks than you can name. Some are small, like the Alpha Group. Others are large, like the Advisor's Network which has more than 250 members across the country. The reason for the explosion in study groups and networks is that independent investment advisors want them because they find value in them. Simply put, independent advisors want the value-added benefits these affiliations offer.

The numbers confirm these trends. In our recent poll of 288 independent investment advisors who are currently not members of an advisor network, 21.5% said they are extremely interested in joining or forming a network (see Exhibit 13.1). These investment advisors all said they intended to be members of a network within a year or two.

Another 29.9% reported being very interested in the idea and would likely join or form a network in the near future but have no specific plans as yet. Even more independent investment advisors (34.4%) said they are somewhat interested and would like to learn more about them. On the other hand, just 14.2% of independent advisors said they are not currently interested in affiliating themselves with a network or study group.

Exhibit 13.1 INDEPENDENT ADVISORS ARE INTERESTED IN JOINING A NETWORK

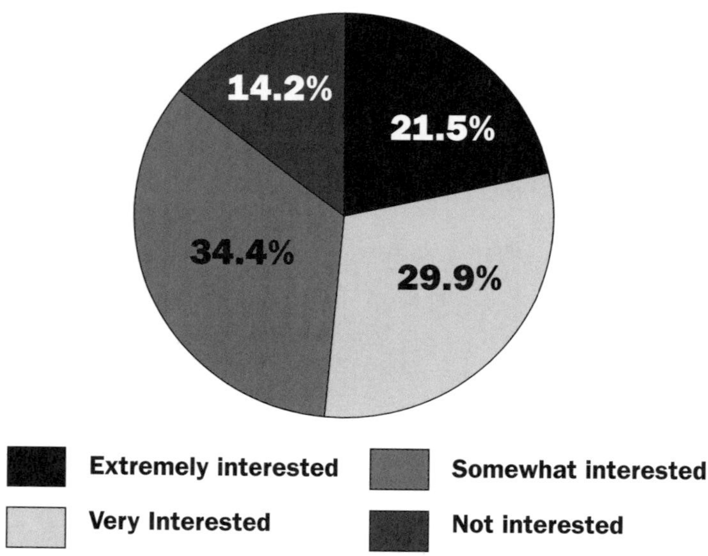

Based on a survey of 288 Independent Investment Advisors

What is interesting is that it is the most successful independent advisors who are the most interested in the additional support for their practices. Of those independent advisors who have gathered more than $30 million in assets, 62.2% are very or extremely interested in joining a network, as compared to 42.9% of independent advisors who have under $30 million under management (see Exhibit 13.2).

Exhibit 13.2 INTEREST IN JOINING A NETWORK BY ASSETS GATHERED

Level of interest	Less than $30 million	$30 million or more
Extremely interested	14.9%	29.9%
Very interested	28.0%	32.3%
Somewhat interested	41.0%	26.0%
Not interested	16.1%	11.8%

Based upon a survey of 288 independent investment advisors

Breaking Through the Production Plateau

Why is there greater interest in networks and study groups among the more successful independent investment advisors? It is because they have hit the production plateau. For many of the more successful advisors, the amount of new assets under management, as a function of the number of clients, has reached a point of equilibrium. That is, they cannot seem to gather net-new-assets; they have hit a plateau. It does not mean that the amount of assets they are responsible for is not growing, but that growth proves to be more a function of investment performance than business development.

Exhibit 13.3 THE PRODUCTION PLATEAU

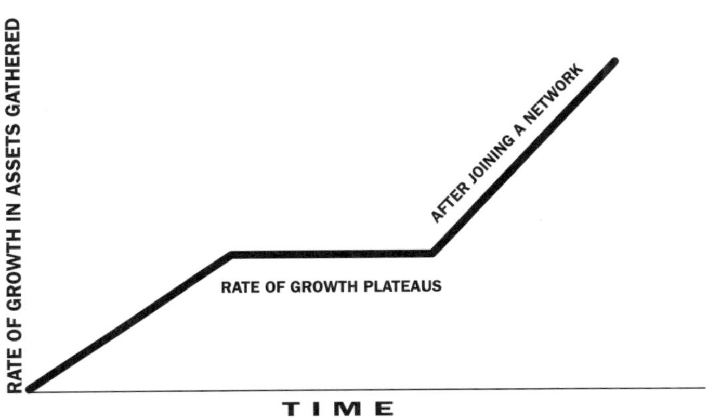

As successful as they are, these investment advisors have just about exhausted their bag of tricks, and their rate of asset gathering is falling off. To get asset growth back on an upward track, these advisors need new ideas, new approaches, new insights. New approaches, ideas and insights are exactly what networks and study groups provide. Since more than half of the most successful investment advisors feel asset growth has plateaued (see Exhibit 13.4), they are turning to networks.

Exhibit 13.4 PERCENT OF ADVISORS WHO FEEL BUSINESS IS PLATEAUING BY ASSETS UNDER MANAGEMENT

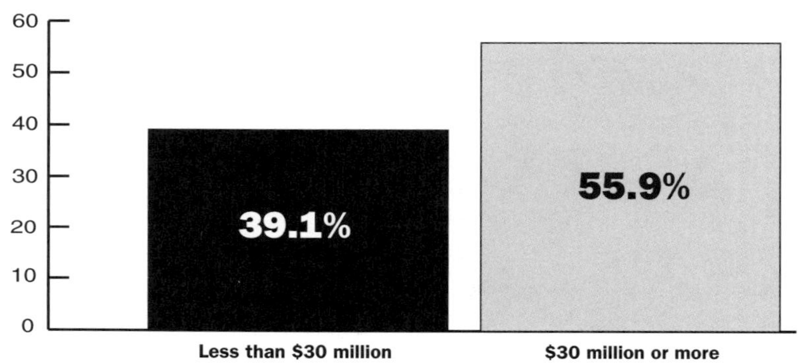

Based upon information from 288 Independent investment advisors

Independent investment advisors with comparatively fewer assets under management do not feel that they have hit the production plateau to the same extent that the more successful independent investment advisors feel they have. While all (100.0%) of the independent investment advisors surveyed want to grow their business by acquiring new clients, the advisors with greater assets under management believe, to a larger degree, that joining a network will help them accomplish this goal.

What to Look for in a Network

The question now becomes, "What makes a network attractive?" Investment advisors seek networks because they cannot find exactly what they are looking for in resource warehouses, broker/dealers, fund companies, associations, investment management firms or consultants.

What independent investment advisors are looking for is information. Strategic, timely, useful information. About one in ten (89.5%) of the advisors surveyed who want to join a network, said that the number one reason was the ability to obtain desired information (see Exhibit 13.5). First and foremost, networks are information resources.

In some industries, associations of independent producers are effective in winning more favorable terms from institutional players. Networks can also play a role in influencing the firms (e.g., broker/dealers, custodial firms, fund companies) that provide services to its members. While this can be a factor, it is minor reason advisors want to join a network. Just about a quarter of independent investment advisors (27.1%) say the ability to influence vendors was an important reason for them to join a network.

Another potential attraction of networks is their image building quality. Being part of a network can enhance your image among other advisors, and can add to your status and prestige. But status and prestige do not turn into clients, so few (9.3%) independent investment advisors see image building as primary reason to join a network.

Exhibit 13.5 INDEPENDENT ADVISORS RATE THE VALUE OF NETWORKS

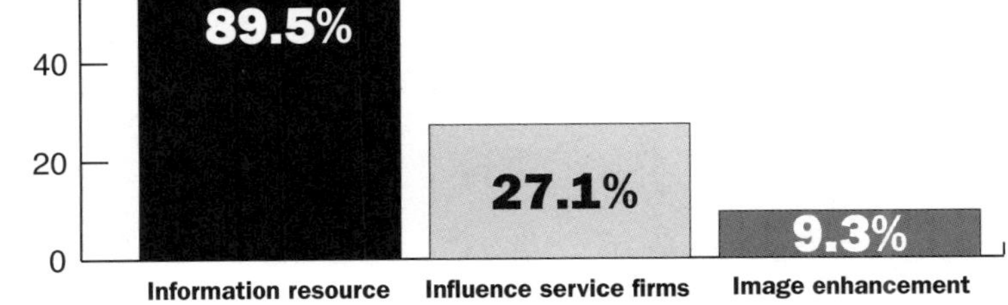

Based upon information from 247 Independent investment advisors

Advisor Networks as Information Resources

Getting better, more usable information is the number one reason independent investment advisors join networks. So let us look a little deeper at exactly what the current information gaps are. To the extent that networks are information resources, it is important to know what types of information are being sought by independent investment advisors. Independent investment advisors have certain expectations about the types of information they are seeking from advisor networks.

The top information stream wanted by independent investment advisors is information about marketing (see Exhibit 13.6). Three out of four (and remember, many of these have $30 million or more under management already), 77.4%, of advisors are looking for insight into how to prospect for new clients, how to effectively position their services and how to manage relationships with existing clients. Considering the commodity nature of investment management products, marketing proficiency is one of the most significant differences between the best of the best advisors and those less successful. The more successful advisors are actually more interested in marketing information than those with fewer assets under management (85.8% compared to 70.8%).

Portfolio management strategies also interest independent investment advisors (64.2%). Portfolio management entails the latest thinking about portfolio theory. This is the type of information for which continuing education credit is awarded. Once again, the more successful independent investment advisors want state-of-the-art thinking about portfolio construction (75.6% compared to 55.3%).

Next in importance comes technology (59.4%). Technology is the cornerstone of the independent investment advisor movement. It is also the most important dynamic impacting the investment management business. Advisors care about being up-to-date when it comes to technology.

Industry intelligence is of considerable interest to about half (53.1%) of independent advisors surveyed. The changes occurring in the industry are occurring at a quicker and quicker pace. Advisors share the most current information with each other through advisor networks and study groups.

Investment research is an important area to 42.7% of those surveyed. Practice management is of interest to some advisors (22.6%), while compliance issues are important to 9.4%.

Exhibit 13.6 INFORMATION DESIRED BY ASSETS UNDER MANAGEMENT FROM ADVISOR NETWORKS

Category	Less than $30 million	$30 million or more	Total
Marketing	70.8%	85.8%	77.4%
Portfolio management	55.3%	75.6%	64.2%
Technology	60.9%	57.5%	59.4%
Industry intelligence	55.3%	50.4%	53.1%
Investment research	41.0%	44.9%	42.7%
Practice management	25.5%	18.9%	22.6%
Compliance	11.2%	7.1%	9.4%

Based upon a survey of 288 independent investment advisors

Industry Associations Do Not Deliver Enough — Yet

Independent investment advisors surveyed were also polled on the ability of industry associations to provide the information they are seeking. Associations such as the International Association for Financial Planning, the National Association of Personal Financial Advisors, and the Institute for Certified Financial Planners are all seeking to position themselves to the independent investment advisor community.

The advisors feel that, at the present time, these and similar associations are not providing them with the quality of information that will enable them to be more successful (see Exhibit 13.7). The more successful advisors, those managing $30 million or more, see less value in the associations than those who are managing fewer assets.

Advisors feel that the information the various associations provide is often not focused enough or updated enough. Associations are already responding with new programs designed to boost the effectiveness of their members. As the industry grows, the associations will become even more responsive to their constituencies.

Exhibit 13.7 PERCENT OF ADVISORS WHO AGREE ASSOCIATIONS DO NOT DELIVER ENOUGH–YET

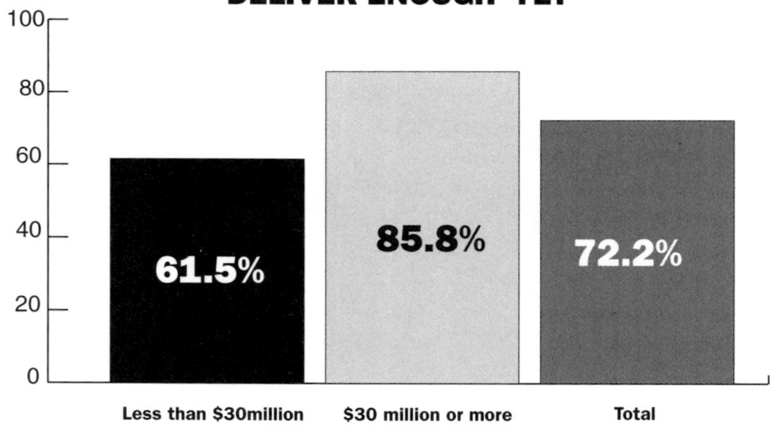

Based upon information from 288 Independent investment advisors

Even though the associations will become a more viable source of information, the advisor networks will nevertheless become a likely staple of the independent investment advisor industry. The association will provide broad-based industry intelligence as well as innovative ideas. The advisor networks will provide more nuts-and-bolts information that is pertinent to a select group of advisors.

Lessons From The Insurance Industry

As noted earlier, the structural dynamics of the world of the high-end insurance agent mirrors what is happening in the world of the independent investment advisors. We can get a preview of how investment advisor networks might evolve by looking over into the insurance industry.

Insurance Agent Study Groups

For the moment, the best parallel to independent investment advisors networks are insurance agent study groups. In these groups, insurance agents get together to discuss the best ways to position various insurance services, how to manage their practices, the changes impacting the insurance industry, the latest tax laws, and so forth.

Study groups are a long-standing educational strategy in the insurance industry because they are extremely effective in enabling insurance agents to grow their businesses. Insurance agents who are participants in study groups generate 2.2 times more annual revenue than the agents who are not in study groups. Study groups are a powerful means of making insurance agents more successful.[1]

It is interesting to know that all insurance industry study groups are not the same. In the insurance industry, there are the vast majority of study groups and the top-of-the-line study groups (often referred to as expert study groups). The members of expert study groups produce 8.2 times more business than insurance agents who were not members of a study group and 4 times more business than insurance agents who were members of a regular study group.

What distinguishes a expert study group? It turns out that there are five critical factors (see Exhibit 13.8):[2]

- The degree of structure in the study group. Expert study groups are much more highly structured. There is a clear mission, set of goals and agenda that are adhered to. Regular study groups tend to be more informal and less structured.

- The use of interactive training methodologies. Expert study groups use methods for processing information that are based on the ways adults learn. They use a high degree of interaction. Regular study groups often rely on the lecture or discussion format.

- The use of outside presenters. Expert study groups regularly bring in recognized authorities on a wide range of topics to help them become more productive. Regular study groups go outside for speakers less often.

- Whether there is a market or product focus. Expert study groups focus on markets as well as products. Expert study groups tend to be formed around markets. Regular study groups emphasize products.

- Use of technology. E-mail is characteristic of expert study groups. Some expert study groups are setting up their own intranets. While these nets are established in conjunction with an insurance carrier or a broker/dealer, they are the domain of the study group and restricted to its members.

Exhibit 13.8 COMPARING HIGH-PERFORMING AND TRADITIONAL STUDY GROUPS

Characteristic	Expert Study Group	Traditional Study Group
Degree of structure	High	Moderate to Low
Use of interactive training methodologies	High to Moderate	Low
Use of outside presenters	Frequently	Occasionally
Focus	Products and Markets	Primarily Products
Technology	E-mail and intranets	Fax and phone

Source: Prince, R.A., "Study Group Participation Increases Income of Agents." National Underwriter, 99 (38) 1996.

As more and more independent investment advisors form or join networks, they should look to the insurance industry for models. It is likely that independent investment advisor networks will resemble expert study groups. In the future, advisors may very well use technology to form virtual expert study groups.

As advisor networks evolve, they will look increasingly like insurance industry producer groups.[3] That is, they will become more influential over the activities, including compensation issues, of the resource warehouses. Advisor networks might even be structured to leverage the equity markets[4] or at least be positioned to sell the network to a financial institution.

Going Forward

- Networks of independent investment advisors are here to stay. More than that, they will be one of the dominant ways advisors organize themselves.

- Networks are seen as an information resource. Advisors get information from networks they cannot obtain from other sources such as resource warehouses.

- The way advisor networks operate is quite close to how study groups work in the insurance industry. By taking the best practices of insurance agent study groups — especially high-performing study groups — advisor networks can substantially enhance their value to its members.

- As advisor networks grow in significance, look for them to influence:

  – Resource warehouses.

  – Investment products development.

  – Compensation issues.

$

[1] Prince, R.A., "Study Group Participation Increases Income of Agents." National Underwriter, 99 (38) 1996.

[2] ibid.

[3] The three defining characteristics of producer groups is that they are composed of a number of independent high-end insurance agents and/or firms, that they negotiate special commission rates with insurance companies and that there are some minimum production requirements. Beyond these three characteristics, producer groups can, and generally do, differ in significant ways. For more information concerning producer groups see: Prince, R.A. "Producer Groups' Lure Goes Beyond Compensation." National Underwriter. 99 (43) 1995; Prince, R.A. "Producer Groups Garner More Interest From Agents." National Underwriter. 101 (6) 1997; Prince, R.A. "The World of Producer Groups." Probe, 44 (2) 1997; Prince, R.A. "The Future of Producer Groups." Probe, 44 (3) 1997.

[4] Prince, R.A. "When Producer Groups Go Public." Probe, in press.

5

Build Your Business III: Own the Affluent Market

14

High-Net-Worth Psychology

"The rich are different from you and me."
-F. Scott Fitzgerald

"People are fascinated by the rich; Shakespeare wrote plays about kings not beggars."
- Dominick Dunne

You know not all of your affluent clients are alike. Some clients love being involved in every detail of investing. Other clients want you to make the decisions. Some clients like innovative new approaches, some like the tried and true. Some clients want to create a pool of wealth for future generations of their family. Other clients want to spend their wealth now.

The secret to building a $100 million or more investment advisor business that thrives irrespective of the ups and downs of the stock market is to truly understand and use high-net-worth psychology. High-net-worth psychology provides a window onto the way affluent investors think and, more importantly, feel about investing. These insights will enable you to more effectively prospect, sell and adroitly manage your relationships with affluent investors.

Market Segmentation

Because markets are not uniform, we segment them. Segmentation involves breaking down a big market into smaller groups that buy and use products and services in similar ways. A good segmentation of a market will sub-divide it into a workable number of groups. You should be able to identify what segment each person falls into fairly easily. Once you know the segment, you will know exactly how to position your investment advisory services, how much hand-holding the clients needs and the like. Segmenting the affluent investor market means you can focus your efforts to get the greatest returns relatively quickly.

There are many ways to segment the affluent investor market. You could segment it by source of wealth, age, income, sex and (or) geography. However, these factors actually have limited value in creating groups of different investors because the affluent are pretty similar in these ways.

As you know, most affluent investment decision-makers live in affluent areas (think of Fairfield County, Connecticut; the Palm Beach area in Florida; Beverly Hills in California and many more). Affluent decision makers are generally male and married. Affluent decision makers are old enough to have accumulated assets. They still have estate and trust decisions to make. Most are between the ages of 45 and 65. Affluent investment decision makers have made their money by owning businesses, owning professional firms or being senior corporate executives. A few inherited wealth.[1] While there are younger rich people, rich women and rich families living outside areas of concentrated wealth, you will agree that the affluent are fairly homogeneous when it comes to demographics.

And yet, they are very different as people, and most importantly, as investors. Even when they match up very closely on demographics, affluent investors can still be light years away from each other on their investment psychology.

That is why high-net-worth psychology is so important. Understanding the psychology affluent investors use when they select their advisors and when they make investment decisions will let you market financial products and services most successfully.

We have explored issues of high-net-worth psychology for many years and have published extensively on it in trade and academic journals. We started by limiting our research to the types of investors most advisors would love to have as clients. Every investor we interviewed or worked with in the course of this research had liquid assets of at least $400,000 (most had over $1 million and the range went up to significantly over $10 million)[2]. All had discretionary investment accounts. All used professional investment advisors.[3]

To identify the high-net-worth psychology of affluent investors, we reviewed everything written about the wealthy. We interviewed and surveyed several thousand affluent investors over several years. Most importantly, we tested our ideas in the field, working closely with an array of financial advisors and financial and legal institutions across the country. Over the course of many years of going back and forth between the field and research studies, we identified the nine profiles of wealth.

The Nine Profiles of Wealth

The nine profiles we discovered as a result of these many years of experiments and research are nine distinct psychological types of affluent investors.[4] Here is a thumbnail sketch of each:

- **Family Stewards** feel that the purpose of investing is to let them take proper care of their families.
- **Financial Phobics**[5] hate being involved in investment decisions. They completely rely on investment advisors to take care of things.
- **Independents** think investing is a necessary evil.
- **The Anonymous** are very secretive and believe investment success is crucial for their personal comfort.
- **Moguls** identify investing as a means of attaining personal power.
- **VIPs** like the status that successful investing can generate.
- **Accumulators** simply want to be rich.
- **Gamblers** treat investing as a very enjoyable hobby.
- **Innovators** desire to be on the cutting edge of investment technology.

Most investment advisors who have familiarized themselves with high-net-worth psychology find they can use it quickly. They also find that high-net-worth psychology gives them the insights to use their resources most efficaciously. By understanding high-net-worth psychology you can position your services expertly. Furthermore, your prospecting and relationship management efforts will be much more effective.

Some of the psychological types are common to more investors than others.[6] Family Stewards are the most common type of affluent investor, representing 20.7% of all affluent investors. Innovators are fairly rare; just 5.5% of all affluent investors. Exhibit 14.1 shows the percentage of affluent investors represented by each psychological type.

Exhibit 14.1 PERCENT OF EACH AFFLUENT PSYCHOLOGY

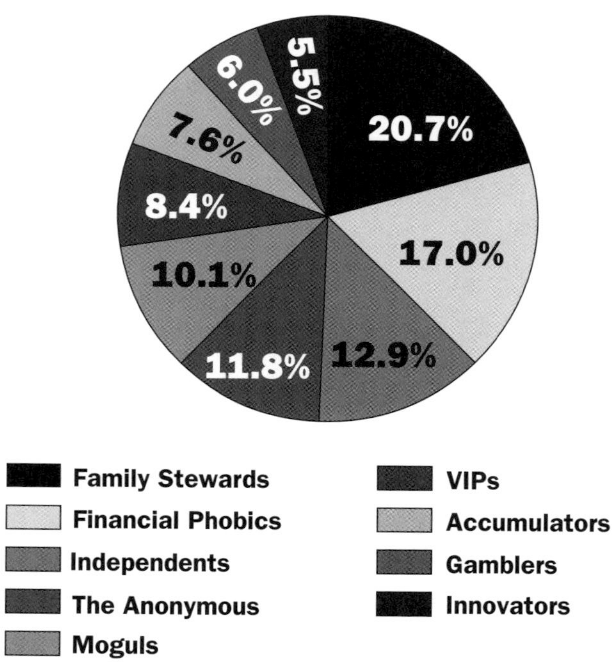

Source: Prince, R.A., & File, K.M. Cultivating the Affluent: How to Segment and Service the High-Net-Worth Market. N.Y.: Institutional Investor, 1995.

We have found that different financial providers attract different types of investors.[7] For example, the generally more conservative private banking divisions of money center banks attract more than their share of Family Stewards and Financial Phobics. The psychological types prefer different investment products as well. Innovators want to learn about the newest products. Many hedge fund investors are Innovators (along with VIPs and Accumulators).[8]

High-Net-Worth Psychology and Assets

Another way investors vary is with respect to assets under management. Innovators average the highest investable assets per clients, perhaps because of their aggressive approach coupled with their understanding and use of the latest investment rocket science. Family Stewards have significant assets, in part because they are so frugal.[9]

Exhibit 14.2 HIGH-NET WORTH PSYCHOLOGY AND ASSETS

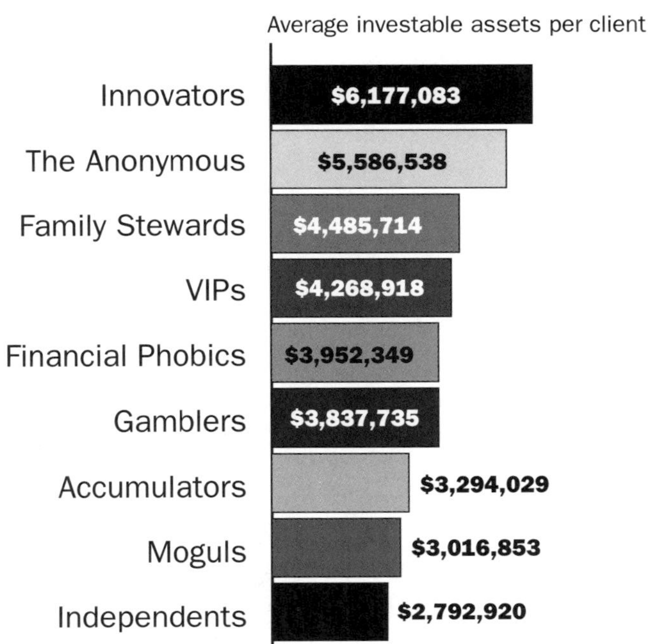

Source: Prince, R.A., & File, K.M. Cultivating the Affluent: How to Segment and Service the High-Net-Worth Market. N.Y.: Institutional Investor, 1995.

High-Net-Worth Psychology and Investment Orientation

As you can now expect, the investment orientation, risk tolerance and relative investment expertise of each segment is very different (see Exhibit 14.3).[10]

Family Stewards are naturally more conservative because they want to conserve assets for the next generation. They therefore usually have a low risk tolerance, and are adverse to new (complex) investing paradigms because their expertise is moderately low.

Financial Phobics are also very conservative, to the extent they are involved at all, in terms of their investment orientation. Financial Phobics usually have a very low risk tolerance and very very low level of investment expertise. They lean, almost completely, on their financial advisors.

Independents tend to have a mid-range investment orientation, which pairs well with a moderate risk tolerance. Independents often still feel slightly uncomfortable with anything too contemporary as their investment expertise is a little below average.

The Anonymous investors prize confidentiality and financial information security above all else. They are ordinarily conservative in investment orientation and have a low risk tolerance. Their level of personal knowledge is generally low, because they are not very open about their concerns which tends to limit their ability to gather new significant information.

Moguls seek personal power and influence. Money is an effective way of achieving power, so Moguls value the investment management process. Moguls are often fairly aggressive in terms of their investment orientation because they want high returns. Their risk tolerance, however, is usually low. They fear losing relative power. They are only moderately expert in investing, although unlikely to ever acknowledge their shortcomings.

VIPs value the respect and esteem of others. Investing is another way for them to achieve their status needs, and like investment advisors who make them feel important. VIPs usually have a moderate risk profile and are only moderately knowledgeable.

Accumulators want to be personally wealthy. As a result, they are frequently aggressive investors with a high tolerance for risk. They are also fairly knowledgeable about investing, and receptive to ideas from financial advisors who understand their needs.

Gamblers relish the excitement and joy of risk-taking (and winning). They, too tend to be aggressive investors, and they are very high in terms of personal investment expertise. This is the group that sees investing as a hobby. They have strong opinions.

Innovators like to hold positions in whatever is the newest investment vehicle. They are technically adept, and like to be the first among their peer group to be in the know. They are frequently very aggressive investors and have a high risk tolerance as a result.

Exhibit 14.3 HIGH-NET WORTH PSYCHOLOGY AND INVESTMENT ORIENTATION

Segment	Investment Orientation	Risk Tolerance	Investment Expertise
Family Stewards	Conservative	Low Moderate	Moderately Low
Financial Phobics	Very Conservative	Very Low	Very Low
Independents	Moderate	Moderate	Moderately Low
The Anonymous	Conservative	Low	Low
Moguls	Aggressive	Moderate	Moderate
VIPs	Moderate	Moderate	Moderate
Accumulators	Very Aggressive	High to Moderate	Moderate
Gamblers	Aggressive	High	Very High
Innovators	Very Aggressive	High	Very High

High-Net-Worth Psychology and Loyalty

Because of their different psychologies and their approach to investing, affluent investors have a different degree of loyalty to their financial advisors.[11] Family Stewards, and The Anonymous are extremely loyal. Family Stewards are loyal because they regularly think of their advisors as "family," and The Anonymous are loyal because they are unwilling to disclose personal information to anyone else. Financial Phobics are also extremely loyal because of their lack of ability to discern coupled with their disinterest in comparison shopping.

Moguls, VIPs and Accumulators are relatively loyal because their advisors are the means by which they attain their goals. The other segments are relatively low in loyalty.

Exhibit 14.4 INVESTOR PSYCHOLOGY AND LOYALTY TO ADVISORS

Family Stewards	Very High
Financial Phobics	Very High
Independents	Moderately Low
The Anonymous	Very High
Moguls	High
VIPs	High
Accumulators	High
Gamblers	Low
Innovators	Moderate

We have written a more exhaustive treatment of high-net-worth psychology in Cultivating the Affluent, and so will not repeat the discussion here. This chapter was intended to only introduce high-net-worth psychology to those who have not yet read that book. The next several chapters include many examples of high-net-worth psychology. They show how you can use high-net-worth psychology to build your business.

We have found investment advisors learn high-net-worth psychology very quickly. They can immediately name clients who fit many (if not all) the profiles. Investment advisors learn the segment names quickly. They are also able to "get under the skin" of each psychology type, so that they can comfortably predict behavior, anticipate investment interests and respond to needs.

Going Forward

- There are nine investor psychology types:
- Family Stewards feel that the purpose of investing is to let them take proper care of their families.

- Financial Phobics hate being involved in investment decisions. They completely entrust others, such as investment advisors, to take care of things.
- Independents think investing is a necessary evil.
- The Anonymous are very secretive and believe investment success is crucial for their personal comfort.
- Moguls identify investing as a means of attaining personal power.
- VIPs like the status successful investing can generate.
- Accumulators simply want to be rich.
- Gamblers treat investing as a very enjoyable hobby.
- Innovators desire to be on the cutting edge of investment technology.

- Each psychological type has a different investment orientation.
- Each psychological type also has a different level of trust in their investment advisors, and are naturally more or less loyal to their investment advisors.
- High-net-worth psychology enables you to work more effectively with affluent investors.

$

[1] Prince R.A. & File K.M., Marketing to the Affluent: A Toolkit for Life Insurance Professionals. OH: National Underwriter, 1995.

[2] In our research on family offices, the starting point was liquid assets of $50 million. Some of the families had liquid assets of over $200 million. A few even reached the $1 billion level.

[3] Prince, R.A., & File, K.M. Cultivating the Affluent: How to Segment and Service the High-Net-Worth Market. N.Y.: Institutional Investor, 1995.

[4] The initial program of research dealt with discretionary investment accounts. Subsequent research has addressed a variety of products such as hedge funds, private equity investments and Wrap accounts. The model has also been employed in obtaining a more extensive understanding family offices. These findings have been presented in various issues of Private Asset Management a newsletter of Institutional Investor.

[5] Initially Financial Phobics were referred to as Investment Phobics because the focus of the research was solely on investment services. However, as we have expanded our research programs to other financial and related services and products (e.g., life insurance, asset protection planning, etc.) coupled with our experience working with high-end producers as well as financial institutions we have found that this personality avoids financial dealings if at all possible. When it is impossible to avoid financial issues, they mentally distance themselves. Thus, we now recognize this segment to be adverse to all financial issues not just investment issues. Therefore, we modified the name to reflect this understanding.

[6] Prince, R.A., & File, K.M. Cultivating the Affluent: How to Segment and Service the High-Net-Worth Market. N.Y.: Institutional Investor, 1995.

[7] While there has been a "historic" attraction by different affluent investor personalities to different types of financial institutions, as we discussed in the first section, it is the individual advisor who develops a strong relationship with the affluent investor that commands the day. With dramatic structural changes transforming the financial services industry, those advisors and institutions that best understand these changes and take appropriate action will be the ones that will build enduring successful investment advisory businesses.

[8] Prince, R.A., & File, K.M. Cultivating the Affluent: How to Segment and Service the High-Net-Worth Market. N.Y.: Institutional Investor, 1995.

[9] ibid.

[10] ibid.

[11] This discussion on loyalty is predicated on investment advisors doing very little to build meaningful personal bonds with their affluent clients. As we will see, loyalty can be significantly enhanced by being appropriately responsive. High-net-worth psychology is a tool that can help you be more in tune with your affluent clients. We have documented that those investment advisors who employ high-net-worth psychology in conjunction with high-impact relationship management create exceptionally loyal affluent investor clients.

15

Power Prospecting Strategies

"When it is a question of money, everyone is of the same religion."
- Voltaire

"The good news is that the rich — whether old or new, entrepreneur or inheritor, famous or infamous, all have at least one thing in common: their behavior is a spectator sport."
- Jon Winokur

Prospecting is the single most difficult hurdle for financial professionals to face.[1] Frankly, most affluent investors are just not in the market for a new investment advisor. As much as you are looking for them, they are not looking for you.

Prospecting is hard because affluent investors often already have advisors, and/or a way of managing their assets that works for them. In addition, the affluent are gun-shy. Affluent people know from experience that they are the most attractive customer for everything, and that everyone is trying to get their business. Investment advisors solicit the affluent all the time. The affluent do not like it. They know how to avoid it.

All this means that the most difficult part of an investment advisor's job is finding prospective clients. More specifically, the difficult part is finding qualified prospective affluent investors. What qualifies an affluent investor? They are the (very few) wealthy individuals who want to talk to you about your investment advisory services.

When it comes to getting in front of a qualified affluent prospect, everything you can probably think of can work, and, in the right situations, work well. For instance, certain well-structured direct mail programs are quite effective in generating qualified leads. The right kind of highly focused and properly placed advertising has sometimes attracted qualified wealthy prospects.

Since each of the many approaches to prospecting can be effective under the right circumstances, you should evaluate each in the context of your firm's marketing plan. Given your current market position and strategy, you will create a mix of prospecting approaches.[2]

Our research has, however, revealed that there are three prospecting strategies that are especially effective.[3] We call them the power prospecting strategies, and they are:

- Client referrals.
- Referrals from intermediaries.
- Seminars.

Client Referrals[4]

Obtaining referrals to affluent prospects from your current clients is the single most effective way to build your business. It is sometimes slow going, but it works very well.

Of course, only your most highly satisfied affluent clients will want to refer their friends and associates to you. So your first step in prospecting is to make sure that your current affluent investors are as highly satisfied as you can make them.[5]

Our data shows the power of satisfied clients. Dissatisfied clients are unlikely to make referrals, every 100 dissatisfied clients results in just 15 referrals for their advisors.[6] You can almost double this referral rate if your clients are all satisfied. Every 100 satisfied clients results in 26 new client referrals for their advisors. But, as Exhibit 15.1 shows, the real payoff is in making current clients VERY satisfied. Every 100 very satisfied clients results in 66 new client referrals for their advisors. If all those clients came to you, that's a 66% growth rate in your client base in a single year. For most advisors, that kind of growth means never doing any other form of prospecting.

Exhibit 15.1 NUMBER OF NEW CLIENT REFERRALS PER 100 CURRENT CLIENTS IN A YEAR

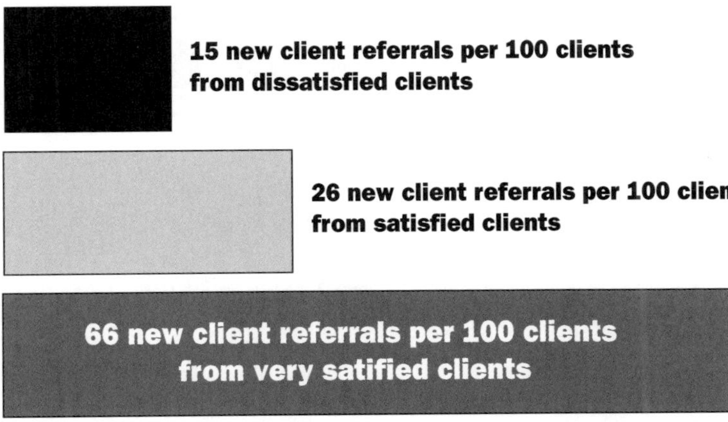

Source: Prince, R.A., & File, K.M. Cultivating the Affluent: How to Segment and Service the High-Net-Worth Market. N.Y.: Institutional Investor, 1995.

Client referrals also come because advisors ask for them. We studied a lot of how the best of the best financial advisors managed these very high client referral rates. It turn out they all use a similar process. We have boiled down that process into seven steps for you. Apparently there are no great secrets to asking for and getting client referrals. It is a process that any investment advisor can use. The seven steps are:

Step #1: Set the stage for soliciting feedback

Step #2: Solicit feedback after significant interactions

Step #3: Client review of the relationship

Step #4: Ask for the referral

Step #5: Thank them for the referral

Step #6: Tell them what happened

Step #7: Thank them again

As we noted, these seven steps emerged from intensive studies of the best of the best. You can build a $100 million investment advisory business following these seven steps, but you need to add your own spin. The seven steps are a framework for you to adapt. Your own personality and individual style will make the framework unique to you. As you become more skilled at obtaining affluent client referrals, continue to modify the seven step framework to create a personal approach that works best for you.

Step #1: Set Expectations

From the very beginning of your relationship with each and every affluent client, you need to prepare them for providing feedback. You need feedback from your clients in order to know whether they are as satisfied as they could be.

Create the right set of client expectations from the very beginning of every relationship. From the start, explain to your affluent investors you will be checking in frequently to see how satisfied they are. Part of creating the policy statement involves setting the stage for soliciting feedback. Let them know they can expect you to ask how things went after every significant interaction and at periodic intervals.[7]

The best of the best also take the time at the beginning of the relationship to let their clients know that they appreciate referrals. The best investment advisors find that some clients generate several referrals a year each. Perhaps this new client was a referral; that is a perfect opening to create expectations for later referrals.

Step #2: Solicit Feedback After Significant Interactions

As you have already set the stage for receiving feedback on client satisfaction, you can now readily obtain it. When do you want feedback?

As you work with affluent investors, there will be crucial points in the relationship that are best for obtaining feedback. Ask for feedback after you have performed a major service for the client. Good times are after a significant increase in the value of the portfolio, after completion of a planning process, after investing new assets, and after rebalancing the portfolio. After each significant interaction, it is important that you solicit feedback.

Obviously, the best feedback is a compliment. These are gratifying to hear, and pleasant for all concerned. Talk with the client until you find at least one thing you can improve upon in a tangible way, and then to act on that improvement. Above all, do not be afraid of negative feedback. Many affluent investors understand that market volatility and back office mistakes are inevitable. What they look for is your commitment to work intensely on their behalf. Investors understand that things can go wrong, and look for your efforts to make them right. Often the most satisfied clients are the ones who have been through difficult periods with you.

Step #3: Client Review of the Relationship

Set aside the time for a periodic review with each affluent client. Review investment performance and other events in the account. Then review the relationship by soliciting feedback again. This step enables you to get an exact fix on client satisfaction and to gauge the strength of the relationship. Once you know your affluent client is very satisfied, move to Step #4.

Step #4: Ask for the Referral

Frankly, it is rare for a wealthy investor to wake up one morning and think about providing a referral to one of their investment advisors. You have to take the initiative if you want the referral.

The best of the best tell us that just asking affluent clients if they know of someone who can use their services is not very effective. They often get no for an answer. This approach generally fails because you are making your affluent clients deal with two issues simultaneously. You are asking them who might need your investment services and whether or not they would feel comfortable with making a referral of that person. You can increase your effectiveness by separating these two questions.

Using high-net-worth psychology can make you considerably more effective in how you ask for referrals. Talk about the benefits of your investment services from the perspective of the affluent individual. Wealthy investors tend to know other investors of the same psychological type.[8] Focus on high-net-worth psychology and their reasons for investing. You can better customize your approach to asking for the referral this way. For example, you could review all the steps you take to safeguard confidentiality with an investors who fits The Anonymous personality type; then ask if they would feel comfortable referring you to others who value the same sort of safeguards.

Step #5: Thanking Them for the Referral

The thing to recognize is that there is social cost to your affluent clients for providing you with a referral. So you should reciprocate, quickly, with shows of gratitude. A quick handwritten note, for example, is essential. George Bush was famous for his handwritten notes, and this personal touch made him popular among politicians and world leaders.

Thanking your affluent clients for referrals provides you with another opportunity to maintain contact. You are also intensifying your relationship with them.

Step #6: Providing Process Feedback

Your affluent client (the one that made the referral) will be curious how things went with the people they referred to you. It is critical that you let them know, but be very mindful about confidentiality.

One of the first things your client will want to know is whether or not you were able to make contact with the affluent person. They also want to know if the initial meeting went well. One way to provide process feedback is to send your client another quick note. Notes are better than telephone calls because they do not have to be returned (and you can avoid playing telephone tag). Of course, you will want to make some of these follow-up contacts over the phone in order to explore whether any new needs have arisen as well as to build on your existing relationship.

It is critically important to protect the confidentiality of the affluent prospect. Never disclose personal information or the business of one client to another.

Step #7: Thank Them Again

Just because you thanked your affluent client for the referral once, do not stop there. Thank them again. Especially thank them if you close some business.

Intermediary Referrals[9]

Many other types of advisors — accountants, attorneys and insurance agents — work with the affluent. Their services compliment yours. We refer to these other types of advisors as intermediaries, because they are in an intermediate position between you and the affluent investors who are their clients for other services.[10] There are specific actions that you can take that will enable you to generate a stream of high-quality referrals from intermediaries such as accountants, attorneys and insurance agents.

Of course, some insurance agents and accountants are your competitors, or are considering being your competitors.[11] Clearly, intermediaries who are active in investment management will not work effectively with you. Many of these professionals will not get into investment advisory services, and they want to work with you.

To be successful in getting affluent investor referrals from intermediaries, you need to understand their requirements. You need to take their needs into account, both when designing channel development strategies and when implementing them. Over the long term, new affluent investor referrals will go to the investment advisors who create referral systems that fit in with the professional cultures of accountants, attorneys, and insurance agents.

Who To Target

Even among those intermediaries who are not seeking to become investment advisors, there are factors you should know. In other words, certain insurance agents, accountants and attorneys are better candidates to provide you with affluent investor referrals than others.

Insurance agents who are just building their practices are a better target than the well-established insurance agents. Younger insurance agents have not fixed their allegiance to a few investment advisors, and are very interested in anything that will help them build their practices. Investment advisors can tap into younger successful insurance agents in one of three ways. You can work through wholesalers. You can target producer groups and insurance brokerage networks. You can target individual agents.

On the other hand, you should target attorneys and accountants who are at the peak of their professional years. The accountants to target are those with high incomes who are growing their incomes. These are the accountants who have already established themselves professionally, who have a well-developed client base and who are ready to harvest the efforts of their younger years.

In targeting attorneys, investment advisors should focus their efforts among attorneys who are already making referrals for several reasons. They represent the largest proportion of all attorneys. They are familiar with the purposes of making referrals and some of the benefits of doing so. They are also looking for ways to augment their already successful practices.

Getting Referrals

You have a number of strategies at your disposal for motivating intermediaries to provide referrals. One strategy is compensation, either on a fixed fee basis or as a percentage of assets. Another strategy is reciprocal referrals. Still another is joint marketing program support.

Compensation is not a strategy you should use across the board. Almost all attorneys say they cannot and will not accept compensation as it is a violation of their professional standards. The same is true with many accountants, although in some states accountants can legitimately accept direct compensation for referrals to investment advisors. On the whole, with both attorneys and accountants, this is not the most readily accepted approach. Therefore, investment advisors should usually not offer direct compensation to accountants and attorneys.

On the other hand, insurance agents are able to receive monetary compensation according to the standards of their field, and they understand the value of referrals. Our surveys show that insurance agents prefer monetary rewards when it comes to referral programs.

In working with attorneys and accountants you should offer reciprocal referral and other marketing support opportunities. In establishing reciprocal referral programs, you should be careful that everyone agrees on the frequency of referrals. You need make as many referrals back as they make to you.

Joint marketing programs are an effective means of getting referrals from accountants, attorneys and insurance agents. In joint marketing programs, you and the accountant, attorney or insurance agent prospect for new affluent clients together. For example, you and an attorney may want to hold seminars on charitable estate planning for an investor with a VIP psychology.[12] Clients developed through this process would have legal needs (the establishment of a charitable remainder trust) and investment needs (the assets held in trust). Often these programs entail sharing access to the affluent clients of both parties. We have seen well-structured seminar programs conducted by investment advisors with accountants, attorneys and insurance agents be quite effective.[13]

Enhancing Relationships With Intermediaries

Building a $100 million investment management business by accessing the affluent clientele of intermediaries, will happen one insurance agent, one accountant, or one attorney relationship at a time. Nurture each relationship with an intermediary as carefully as you would nurture each relationship with an affluent investor. In order to cement your relationships with intermediaries, you will have to pay attention to the following six building blocks:

> **Building Block # 1**—Network. The first step in constructing a referral network that will sustain your investment management business for years to come is to develop individual professional relationships with intermediaries.
>
> **Building Block # 2**—Trust. Intermediaries will not make that referral until they feel they can trust you not to damage the relationships they have with their affluent clients.
>
> **Building Block # 3**—Satisfaction. Highly satisfied high-net-worth clients will praise the you to

intermediaries, which will reinforce the tendency among them to refer other wealthy clients.

Building Block # 4—Communications. More investment advisors lose referrals because they fall into the "communications trap" than for any other reason. The "communications trap" occurs when investment advisors do not convey important information to intermediaries.

Building Block # 5—Proactivity. Intermediaries will respond positively to you if you are proactive in keeping them in the loop.

Building Block # 6—Relationships. There are significant and costly consequences to switching from one professional relationship to another. Therefore, intermediaries will generally invest heavily in their relationships with investment advisors. Your challenge is to become the #1 investment advisor for referrals.

Overall, these six building blocks will enable you to create an intermediary referral network that will produce results. The key is consistency when cultivating intermediaries.

Seminar Referrals[14]

We find that many investment advisors make a basic mistake when they put on seminars. They try to sell products. We find, however, that the most effective seminars do not try to sell investment products, services, or investment performance. Instead, they are designed to showcase the investment advisor. In seminars, you have a great opportunity to communicate to your audience of prospective investors that you are a consummate professional. You can let them know you are a trustworthy and skilled expert when it comes to the field of investment management.

We have studied many seminars programs over the years, especially from the point of view of the prospective client. Unfortunately, a great many investment advisors lose selling opportunities in seminars. Quite a few seminars actually work at cross-purposes to their intended objectives. Instead of creating opportunities to work with the wealthy, a poorly designed seminar can end up placing a barrier between the investment advisor and affluent investors.

When you produce a seminar, you want it to be as effective as possible. What constitutes being effective? Since the goal of the seminar is a subsequent one-to-one meeting, then the more effective your seminar, the more prospective wealthy investors you will meet individually. The secret of making this happen is proper planning and execution.

The Importance of Planning

The key to the success of any effective seminar program is planning. Think of the following topics when you plan a seminar for affluent prospects. Make sure to include the following components:

> **Step 1:** What is the seminar about? The first thing you must do is decide what the topic of the seminar is from the point of view of your audience. You may want to sell estate planning, but what a Family Steward is interested in buying is building intergenerational wealth to take care of their family.
>
> **Step 2:** Producing the seminar. To grab and hold the attention of your seminar participants means you have to organize the material in a way that captures their attention. That means the seminar should be interactive and focused on solving financial concerns. It must emphasize benefits, not products.
>
> **Step 3:** Filling the seats. Make sure the right people are in the seats, and you insure the success of the seminar. In our experience, a letter is usually not sufficient (wealthy people receive many such invitations). An invitation from a trusted advisor or associate delivered in person is much more effective.
>
> **Step 4**: Follow-up. The number one objective of a seminar is to enable you to set up one-on-one meetings with affluent prospects. Therefore, it is very important to do everything you can to follow-up with attendees.

The Art of Public Speaking

One of the places we have seen seminars falter is in the presentations themselves. All too often, the caliber of the presenters is less than exceptional. For your seminars, you need to insure that you have presenters who can communicate effectively to a group. High quality public speaking is not a gift. Like most other skills, public speaking can be learned.

Public speaking is an ability that you need to use not only in seminars, but in small group and individual presentations. Therefore, being comfortable with public speaking is a crucial skill for investment advisors who have any client contact.

The direct route to confidence is to make sure your material is first rate. Your material should be accurate and timely, and you should be confident of your mastery of the subject matter. The key to motivating an audience is for you to sincerely believe in what you are saying. By presenting with conviction, you are personalizing the material for each and every member of the audience. Enthusiasm and good organization complete the picture.

Never lose sight of why you are going to the trouble of putting on a seminar. It is to motivate people in the audience to work with you. The presentation is always is a call to action. The seminar must inspire the audience. It must motivate them to take the initiative to work with you.

Going Forward

- Prospecting is one of the most challenging tasks of independent investment advisors. Your mix of prospecting strategies will depend on your marketing plan.

- Our research has revealed three power prospecting strategies:

  – Client referrals.

  – Referrals from intermediaries.

  – Seminars.

- The single most successful method for prospecting is through client referrals. Clients know other affluent investors, and are willing to recommend you if they like what you have done for them.
  - You should focus on creating very high levels of client satisfaction.
- You should them take advantage of key points in the relationship to obtain feedback and ask for referrals.
  - Follow the seven step client referral generating process and expect the referrals from clients to take time to grow into a steady stream.
- Referrals from intermediaries such as accountants, attorneys and insurance agent can grow a practice:
  - Screen intermediaries to be sure they are not competitors.
  - Follow the building block approach to developing successful relationships with intermediaries.
- Seminar selling is the third key to power prospecting. Seminars are most effective when jointly sponsored by intermediaries.
  - The goal of seminars is to sell yourself, not products.
  - Focus on obtaining a follow-up one-on-one meeting.
  - Follow the four steps to successful seminar selling.

$

[1] Prince R.A. & File K.M., Marketing to the Affluent: A Toolkit for Life Insurance Professionals. OH: National Underwriter, 1995.

[2] Extensive detailed analyses of the internal operations of independent investment advisory firms identifies opportunities for creating prospecting matrices. Depending on a variety of factors such as the investment advisor's services portfolio, these matrices enable the advisor to most effectively employ various prospecting strategies to create a synergistic effect.

[3] Prince R.A. & File K.M., Cultivating the Affluent: How to Segment and Service the High-net-worth Market. N.Y.: Institutional Investor, 1995.

[4] This methodology is adopted from Prince R.A. & File K.M., Marketing to the Affluent: A Toolkit for Life Insurance Professionals. OH: National Underwriter, 1995. It has been modified appropriately. The derivation of these seven steps is based on financial advisors who are especially adept at obtaining client referrals. They grow their financial services practices at a mean rate of 40% new affluent clients per year strictly through referrals.

[5] There are algorithms that investment advisors can use to improve their ability to generate client referrals. These algorithms offer guidance in determining who to ask a referral from; whether it is a peer, a family member, or a friend. No matter who it is, the seven step method is applicable.

[6] These referrals are made because of the exceptional investment performance of the advisor. Unless you can guarantee consistently exceptional investment performance, you should consider high-impact relationship management. Even when you can produce consistently exceptional investment performance, high-impact relationship management is more important to generating new affluent referrals.

[7] Even at this point it is worthwhile to use high-net-worth psychology. Setting the stage for soliciting feedback is best accomplished in the context of the affluent investor's psychology.

[8] Working within a psychological type is significantly more effective than "traditional" target marketing. By obtaining referrals based on psychological type you will dramatically increase your chances of closing business because your affluent client and the wealthy individual you are referred to are usually "in synch" about key financial services including investment management.

[9] The section is based on an extensive analysis of the advisor referral process which appears, in detail, in Prince, R.A., and File, K.M.

Cultivating the Affluent II: Leveraging High-Net-Worth Client and Advisor Relationships. N.Y.: Institutional Investor, 1997. In addition, the section includes the observations and experiences of Prince & Associates in building intermediary referral programs for elite producers. Based on our experience, you must keep in mind that these programs, while certainly one of the most effective means of obtaining qualified leads, is time consuming and requires not only a great deal of energy but a very clear understanding of the psychology of the specific intermediary in question. Furthermore, it requires you be sensitive to the nuances of the situation. We have found that it takes about a year from the initial meeting with the intermediary until referrals start to flow. However, once they start to flow it is not long before you have a gusher.

[10] Another type of intermediary that can be a source of affluent clients are nonprofits. The focus here is on assisting the nonprofits in generating major and planned gifts. However, the way you need to work with nonprofits is vastly different than the steps you need to take in working with other intermediaries. We have found that, depending on your areas of expertise coupled with your knowledge of charitable estate planning, it is not particularly difficult to find fund-raisers who are very interested in working with you.

[11] Attorneys are also considering the investment advisory business. However, at present, all indications are that they will not pose serious competition for some time.

[12] The most successful joint marketing seminars are built around specific affluent investor personalities. Sometimes, depending on the nature of the service being discussed, a few affluent investor personalities can be put in the same room. By building seminars this way you are going to a get optimal results because you are going to "touch" the seminar participants emotionally as well as intellectually.

[13] We have also seen such seminars blow up. To make them work requires taking all action to make any seminar program work (see next section) coupled with creating a smoothly running structure between all the advisors.

[14] This section is adopted from Prince R.A. & File K.M., Marketing to the Affluent: A Toolkit for Life Insurance Professionals. OH: National Underwriter, 1995. It has been modified appropriately.

16

The Relationship Selling Model[1]

"If the rich could hire other people to die for them, the poor could make a wonderful living."
- Yiddish proverb

"Money is a singular thing. It ranks with love as man's greatest source of joy. And with death as his greatest source of anxiety."
- John Kenneth Galbraith

Here's a little quiz. Think back on your last ten warm leads. By warm lead, we mean a qualified affluent prospect. That is, someone who is open to taking on a new investment advisor. Often, warm leads are referrals from current clients or someone in your professional network. Warm leads may come to a seminar you put on. Sometimes, you will turn up a warm lead through your direct marketing.

Of those ten warm leads, how many did you close? Of ten warm leads, how many would the best person in the industry close?

Since it costs so much to create an affluent prospect — a warm lead — it clearly matters how effective we are in converting them into clients. To answer this question, we studied the closing abilities of 4,537 financial advisors, including insurance agents, brokers, private bankers, and investment advisors. We wanted to know industry closing rates as well as get a handle on what the best of the best were doing.

The best of the best will close at least five out of ten warm leads. The best 10% of financial advisors will close five out of ten warm leads. Of course, this doesn't mean closing on managing 100% of a client's portfolio. It does mean having the client place some assets with you, thereby creating a base of business from which you can expand.

Next are the very good closers with a four out of ten closing rate. The very good closers made up 15.2% of the study participants. Nearly half (49.9%) of the financial advisors have a closure rate of three out of ten. This is the industry norm — the industry average. Of course, some investment advisors do not do as well. Those closing two out of ten represent 14.9% of those studied. Lastly, the remaining 9.8% close one out of ten or less.

Exhibit 16.1 CLOSING RATES

Group	Closing Rate	Percent of Advisors
Best of the best	5 out of 10	10.1%
Good closers	4 out of 10	15.2%
Average closers	3 out of 10	49.9%
Below average closers	2 out of 10	14.9%
Poor closers	1 out of 10	9.8%

Based upon information from 4,537 financial advisors

Source: Prince, R.A., & File, K.M. Marketing to the Affluent: A Toolkit for Life Insurance Professionals. OH: National Underwriter, 1995.

We went to school on the best of the best in order to understand what they did to achieve those high closure rates. This research on the best of the best investment advisors has resulted in the development of the relationship selling model. The model is composed on five levels, and each level builds on the one before it:

Professionalism

Professionalism is being ready to succeed. If you want to build a $100 million investment advisory business working with affluent investors, you must commit to being a consummate professional. Professionalism is having the confidence, competence, and client-centeredness to be successful.

Confidence is a can-do mind-set. Confidence is an attitude of achievement. Your frame of mind will make success possible. Confidence is knowing that you will succeed.

Knowing that you will succeed conveys a sense of self-worth when dealing with the affluent. This self-confidence is communicated to others. When you know you will succeed, you exhibit a form of calm self-assurance and personal magnetism.

Exhibit 16.2 THE RELATIONSHIP SELLING MODEL

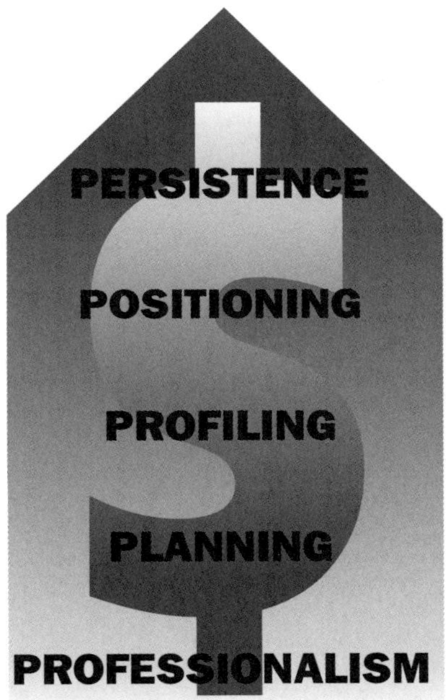

Competence is knowing your investment services. You need to know them inside and out and you need to know how they benefit affluent clients. You need to be benefit oriented. A benefit is a distinct set of definable advantages affluent prospects will receive. Benefits are what the service does. Benefits are what affluent investors gain by going to you. Benefits are what affluent investors buy because they relate to investor psychology.

It is not enough to be competent at managing assets. You have to be competent at communicating the benefits of what you are doing to affluent investors. To communicate benefits, you often have to translate the various features of the investment advisory services you provide into benefits.[2] For example, when working with a VIP, you might show articles in which the portfolio managers have been written up so they can feel associated with investment celebrities. In identifying the benefits of the services and products you provide, it proves useful to take into account high-net-worth psychology.

Client-centeredness is focusing on affluent clients. Being client-centered is doing what is best for clients. In so doing, you will also do what is best for yourself. Central to respect is valuing the uniqueness of the individual. Everyone is special in some way as high-net-worth psychology shows. You must make sure that each affluent prospect and every one of your affluent clients feels special.

Planning

Planning involves having a game plan before meeting with an affluent investor. Of course, you do not know all the answers in advance. But you do have a general approach in mind which you can adjust as you find out more about the situation and the prospective affluent client.

Plan Sales Calls

Preparation makes you that much more able to communicate what you want in a way that will have the greatest impact. Specifically, there are four reasons the best of the best cite for putting in the time and energy to prepare for sales calls:

- Planning increases self-confidence. Being ready and sure of yourself because you know what you are going to say and how you expect to communicate your message makes it that much easier to walk into a meeting with an affluent prospect assured that you will be doing a good job of presenting your case.

- Planning creates a positive sales environment. As you have more and more sales meetings and are more experienced working with each type of affluent investor personality, they see you as someone who truly understands them. This translates into an atmosphere of rapport that enhances the probability of you getting the business.

- Planning communicates professionalism. On-going, solid business relationships are predicated on your knowledge of your potential wealthy clients. Preparing for each sales presentation tells them that you are interested and concerned with them; that you recognize their needs and that you want to do the very best job for them. Planning insures you will use high-net-worth psychology.

- Planning results in increased sales. Careful planning means that you have made the effort to understand what the affluent prospect needs and have skillfully positioned your services to meet those needs. Coupled with the three previously cited reasons the result is a higher success rate.

Four Steps to Exceptional Sales Call Planning

Our research shows that the most successful financial advisors (the top 10%) use four steps to plan for each sales call. As always, we recognize that the four steps overlap, but they do provide a useful framework. The four steps are:

Step 1: Specifying sales call goals. Before you go into each sales meeting, you should know what you want to accomplish. While making the sale is the ultimate goal, there are intermediate objectives for each call.

Step 2: Defining the high-net-worth psychology of the prospect. Here, the nine profiles model of investor psychology is useful.

Step 3: Focus on product and service benefits. You must be prepared to explain the benefits as opposed to the features of your services. These benefits must fit the psychology of the affluent investor. Communicating benefits is good way of focusing on what is important to affluent investors.

Step 4: Development of the sales presentation. Your presentation is the time when you motivate the affluent prospect. You want them to become convinced that the investment advisory services you can provide can meet their needs. They need to believe you are the best source of those financial services.

Profiling

Assessment is where you come to understand the concerns, needs and wants of affluent prospects. Here you actively listen to understand the motivations of the affluent investor with respect to her motivations for investing. The nine profiles of wealth model will provide the means for you to enhance your ability to motivate affluent prospects to become clients.

The Nine Profiles of Wealth

High-net-worth psychology is more effective than other segmentation frameworks such as demographics. Understanding high-net-worth psychology will let you effectively customize your presentations. The nine profiles are the nine distinct psychological types of affluent investors we introduced previously.

Most investment advisors who have familiarized themselves with high-net-worth psychology quickly find that in the process of learning about affluent prospects can identify their investment personalities. If you become comfortable with high-net-worth psychology, you can more effectively position your services.

The Skill of Listening

Investment advisors cannot sell their service to affluent prospects unless they understand what is important to them, what they want to achieve, and what has so far gone unnoticed. Your objective is to help wealthy prospects tell their story from beginning to end. In order to be informed, you have to help affluent prospects open up through effective listening. The skill of listening requires you to trust the process, send appropriate nonverbal cues, listen purposefully and consistently monitor your own feelings. Listening is the key to classifying investors by their psychological type.

There are a number of listening skills that are absolutely essential if you expect to be able to unearth the financial agenda of affluent prospects. "Attending" is the way investment advisors are there with affluent prospects.

The "art of probing" is another skill you need to master. Probes are both questions and statements that solicit information. The adroit interjection of comments can also result in affluent prospects opening up to you. The central aspects of probes include helping affluent prospects tell their story, keeping affluent prospects on track and result in affluent prospects revealing important information.

"Effective questioning" is a cornerstone skill of listening. The very act of questioning demonstrates interest and concern. Usually, open-ended questions are more effective than closed-ended questions.

"Empathy" is an advanced form of listening. Basic listening is about you hearing and understanding what the affluent prospect is saying. When you are being empathic, you are going one step farther, communicating your understanding back to the affluent prospect. Empathy has three components:

- Uncovering the themes in what affluent prospects are saying.
- Focusing on the themes by verifying them.
- Summarizing the themes to communicate that you understand.

Positioning

Strategic positioning involves effectively educating affluent clients to the process of investing; more specifically the process you use in investing their assets. High-net-worth psychology lets investment advisors customize the way they discuss their investment philosophy to affluent investors. Keep in mind that an you are not changing the "way" you invest a wealthy client's assets, but you are adapting how to talk about the "way" you invest because of the financial personality of that affluent client.

There are some specific skill sets you will need to master. These are how to:

- Become influential.
- Teach, do not tell.

- Use stories and anecdotes.
- Involve others.

Become Influential

The best of the best convert prospects to clients through personal influence. Learning how to become influential to your prospects is crucial to success among the affluent. You can do this several ways.

By taking action to be liked, you are creating a personal bond with the affluent investor. Developing specialized knowledge and being recognized for this knowledge makes you an expert. And affluent investors want to work with investment experts. Related to this is being a source of useful information.

Teach, Don't Tell

The best of the best are highly skilled teachers. They have the ability to impart new knowledge, not merely push their services. They are tutoring affluent prospects to the nature of their services.

You must educate affluent prospects about what they are getting always emphasizing the value of your actions in terms of investor psychology. Your presentation skills are critical in each and every sales situation you find yourself. While some of the techniques you will use may change depending on the size of your audience, the substance of what you are doing is the same.

Use Stories and Anecdotes

One of the most powerful ways of teaching is by employing stories and anecdotes. Not only are they effective, they are unobtrusive.

Stories and anecdotes are ways to solve one of the major problems of selling financial services. The problem is this, affluent prospects very much want to work with expert investment advisors. You therefore have to be able to convince wealthy prospects that you are indeed an expert. Stories and anecdotes are accessible ways affluent prospects can gauge the extent to which you understand their problems and issues.

For stories to be effective, you need to make sure they follow the five key storytelling guidelines:

> **Storytelling Guideline 1:** Similarity. The wealthy people in the story need to match the characteristics of your affluent prospects.
>
> **Storytelling Guideline 2:** Relevance. The financial issues faced by the wealthy people in the story must be very close, but not exactly, the same.
>
> **Storytelling Guideline 3:** Applicability. The financial services provided in the story must be comparable to the ones being proposed to affluent prospects.
>
> **Storytelling Guideline 4:** Plot. Good stories have interesting characters, a problem and a resolution.
>
> **Storytelling Guideline 5:** Success. The story must have a happy ending, from the affluent investor's point of view.

Involve Others

Years of researching the financial services purchasing patterns of the affluent repeatedly show the importance of other people on the prospect's decision making process. Generally, because of the importance and impact of financial services on their lives, the affluent will contact other advisors before making a purchase.

Involving others close to the affluent prospect is a three step process:

> **Step 1:** Influencer identification. Determine whose opinions the affluent investor takes into account.
> **Step 2:** Promote influencer involvement. Work to meet with these influencers and keep abreast of what they are saying.
> **Step 3:** Ensure influencer support. Educate the influencers as you would the affluent investor to the value of your services.

Persistence

Closing the sale is essential, yet many financial professionals fail to "ask for the business." Closing the sale involves the use of trial closes, methods for handling objections as well as specific closing techniques.

Trial Closes

Throughout the sales process, the best closers make extensive use of trial closes. The trial close is a means of unobtrusively gauging where you are in making the sale. It is an excellent way of creating a two-way dialogue as well as continuing to involve the affluent prospect in the decision making.

Trial closes let you evaluate how receptive the affluent investor is to what you are discussing. The trial close is a direct question. You use the answer to adjust your sales presentation to the needs of the affluent prospect. Here are a few examples of trial closes:

- How does that sound to you?
- Is this what you were looking for?
- Is this what you wanted to accomplish?
- This is just what you wanted. Isn't it?
- Will this approach be acceptable to your family?

If the affluent investor responds favorably to your trial close, then you are on the right track. You can be confident that the affluent prospect is seriously considering your services, and very soon you should attempt to close.

On the other hand, if you meet with resistance, you know it's not the right time to attempt to close the sale. Somewhere along the line, you missed something crucial. The feedback you receive from trial closes permits you to retrace a few steps and see what you can do to make sure the affluent prospect will commit when you do close.

Handling Objections

Affluent prospects have objections and if you want to close, you must deal with them. You must be able deal with objections throughout the sales process. These are objection management techniques regularly used by the best closers:

- Reframing technique: transform the objection into a question.
- Compensation technique: provide something to offset the objection.
- Social validation technique: obtain independent support to refute the objection.
- Psychological judo technique: turn a negative into a benefit.
- Accuracy correction technique: correct for wrong information or perceptions.
- Forestalling technique: put responding objections off to a later time.

Close to Collect

Closing is the step in the sales process where you help affluent prospects make decisions that will benefit them. The best closers stay flexible when it comes to closing the sale. Different client psychologies lend themselves to different types of closings. Nevertheless, the best of the best all use the following closing techniques:

- Assumptive question closing technique: use questions where you are presuming the affluent investor will use your services.
- Alternate choice closing technique: provide a number of options, all of which result in your services being utilized.
- Summation closing technique: review the affluent prospect's needs and wants and show how you meet them.

- Continuous affirmation technique: the affluent prospect continues to say yes, when you ask for business, he or she says yes.

- Balance sheet close: compare the positives with the negatives.

Once you have attempted a close you should wait for a response. Silence is your ally. Silence works to your benefit. Even though the seconds might seem like hours, you need to wait for the affluent prospect to say something. Speaking will only decrease your chances of an affluent investor deciding to avail himself of your services.

This period of silence is the moment of commitment. If you did a good job up the moment of commitment, the affluent prospect is (at worst) slightly undecided. By waiting for a response you force the decision and the same time you give the prospect the feeling of being in control. Although it might feel like forever, empirical studies show that the moment of commitment is not even sixty seconds (in the laboratory, it is an average of 37 seconds). During the moment of commitment, not only should you not say anything, you should not do anything that may distract the affluent prospect. You should just sit there quietly.

Going Forward

- Relationship selling skills should improve your closing rate.

- The best of the best will close an average of five out of ten warm leads. Some investment advisors close fewer.

- The relationship selling model has five components:

  1. Professionalism. Professionalism is being prepared to succeed.

  2. Planning. Planning is having a general approach in mind that you can adjust as you find out more about the situation and the prospective client.

  3. Profiling. Assessment is where you come

to understand the concerns, needs and wants of affluent prospects.

4. Positioning. Strategic positioning involves educating affluent clients to the process of investing and to the approach you take.

5. Persistence. Closing the sale involves the use of trial closes, methods for handling objections as well as specific closing techniques.

$

[1] The material in this chapter is drawn from the research findings and conclusions found in Prince, R.A., & File, K.M. Marketing to the Affluent: A Toolkit for Life Insurance Professionals. OH: National Underwriter, 1995; Prince, R.A., & File, K.M. Cultivating the Affluent: How to Segment and Service the High-Net-Worth Market. N.Y.: Institutional Investor, 1995.

[2] For many investment advisors a good exercise is to translate features into benefits. You would do this for all the services and products you provide. Once you have mastered this exercise, you can become more sophisticated. That is, you can repeat the exercise, but this time you incorporate the affluent investor personalities into your matrix.

17

High-Impact Relationship Management

"Money, not morality, is the principle of commercial nations."
- Thomas Jefferson

"Money is the lifeblood of the nation."
- Jonathan Swift

By now you know we believe in the importance of relationship management. We think it is the single most important thing you can do to build your business. It is essential if you want to create and maintain a $100 million investment advisory practice.

Relationship management brings you incremental assets to manage (a greater "share of portfolio"). Relationship management brings you new clients through referrals. Relationship management is not just what you do with current clients; relationship management is one of the most effective forms of prospecting you can do.

What is high-impact relationship management? When we ask this question is workshop and seminars, we get a variety of answers. Some say high-impact relationship management is about building rapport. Others say it is about understanding your affluent investors. Still others say it is about creating strong interpersonal and professional bonds with your clients. These answers are all correct, but they are also all incomplete.

Let's stretch these definitions to what you really want. What you really want are loyal affluent clients. Wealthy clients who will stay with you through thick and thin, bear markets as well as bull markets. When you think of relationship management this way, what is it?

We would say high-impact relationship management is those behaviors that result in client retention and client referrals regardless of investment performance.[1]

If you are not growing your affluent client base (through referrals), you are not doing as good a job of relationship management as you could be. We focus on growth (in asset capture) because from the perspective of building your practice, growth is the best outcome of relationship management. In addition, if you focus on growth through clients, you will pay attention to quantitative measures. Quantitative measures give you personal benchmarks that will enable you to significantly build your business.

Over the years, we have investigated the question of what behaviors result in client retention and client referrals regardless of investment performance. In some of our earlier books, we discussed these behaviors in the investor market[2] and in the life insurance market.[3]

In order to understand the specific behaviors important to clients of independent investment advisors, we conducted a two year study of over 400 affluent investors.[4] Over the course of two years we interviewed the investors every quarter. Each time we asked them how their investments did in the preceding quarter as well as how their advisor behaved. We also asked whether they had made any referrals or placed more assets under management with the advisor. We also found out if they switched any or all of their assets to a new advisor and the reason why. This two year perspective allowed us to really understand the specific behaviors that cause clients to stay and the behaviors that cause them to leave.

The results of this study went into the creation of the Business Building Model.

The Business Building Model[5]

And the bottom line is — again — high levels of affluent client satisfaction. To build a growing investment advisor business, you must insure that your affluent clients are as satisfied as can be.

Why is satisfaction so important? We know that highly

satisfied affluent clients will give more assets to you to manage. Additionally, highly satisfied affluent clients will refer other well-heeled investors to you.

The Answer is Client Satisfaction

If affluent clients are highly satisfied, on the average, with investment performance (but not delighted with the interpersonal relationship), they will transfer, to you, an average of 11.8% more assets (see Exhibit 17.1). So, you can expect a client who has entrusted $1 million to you who is highly satisfied with the investment performance (but is not highly satisfied with their personal relationship with you) will add $118,000 to his or her portfolio over a period of two years. Delivering fine investment performance is, therefore, a good asset capture strategy.[6]

But what if you have a client for whom investment performance has been off the mark? Clearly, if you disappoint them with your personal relationship, you can expect no incremental assets from them.

Let's take the third case. Let's take a client who has had disappointing investment results, but who is very satisfied with their relationship with you. Will they add assets to their portfolio? Traditional street wisdom would say no. Affluent clients buy investment performance. But that happens not to be true.[7]

In fact, if your relationship is strong, clients will stay with you even investment performance is off. In fact, such clients will add an average of $96,000 to his or her portfolio to be managed over a period of two years. These results prove relationship management is almost as effective an asset capture strategy as superior investment performance.

Ah ha, you say. What about clients for whom you have been able to bring off excellent investment performance and excellent relationship management. What is the asset capture potential of such clients? This is the most significant result of the research.

It turns out that clients who are happy with both investment performance and the relationship will transfer in the greatest volume of assets — an amount equivalent to more than 20% of the assets already under management. Thus, if you have $1 million dollars of a client's funds, if that client is highly satisfied with both the investment performance of his or her portfolio as well as the quality of the interpersonal relationship, he or she will add an additional $242,000 to be managed within a two year period.

Exhibit 17.1 HIGH CUSTOMER SATISFACTION IS THE BEST ASSET CAPTURE STRATEGY

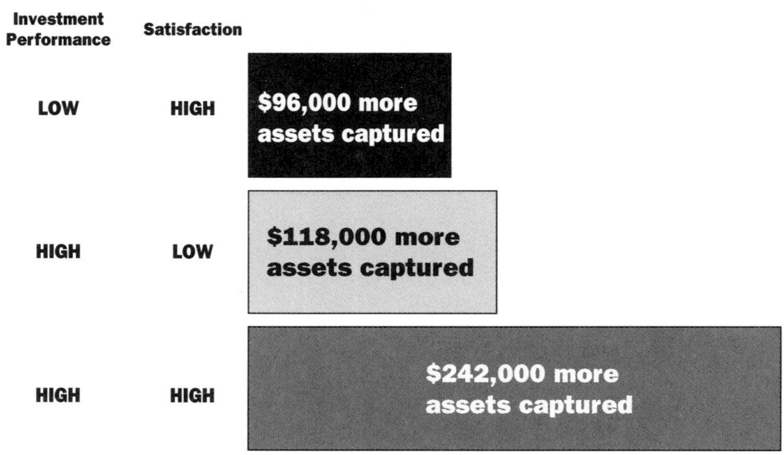

Source: Prince, R.A., and File, K.M. Cultivating the Affluent II: Leveraging High-Net-Worth Client and Advisor Relationships. N.Y.: Institutional Investor, 1997.

Clearly, you have to do both things well for the greatest business building result. The same relationship between investment performance and satisfaction affects client referrals. You must achieve high levels of both investment performance and relationship management in order to achieve the greatest number of referrals from affluent clients. Since the referrals of existing clients are the single most effective way to obtain new clients, these referrals are extremely important.

Affluent clients are reluctant to refer friends and associates of theirs to investment managers whose performance has not been excellent. On the other hand, investment managers who have provided excellent investment performance and relationship management are rewarded with the highest proportion of referrals.

Specifically, wealthy clients who are extremely happy with both aspects of their investment manager's performance say they are almost certain to refer new clients within the next six months (their average probability is 8.7 on a 10 point scale or 87%). Even when investment performance is not especially good, affluent clients will refer their friends and associates if the relationship is very good (probability of 6.8 or 68%).

Affluent clients who are quite satisfied with investment performance are also likely to refer friends and associates (a 3.7 probability or 37%). However, it is not to the extent of those with very strong interpersonal relationships with their investment advisors. And affluent clients who are dissatisfied with both aspects provide the lowest probability of all (0.0 or 0%) — they will not make referrals.

Exhibit 17.2 HIGH CUSTOMER SATISFACTION IS THE BEST CLIENT PROSPECTING STRATEGY

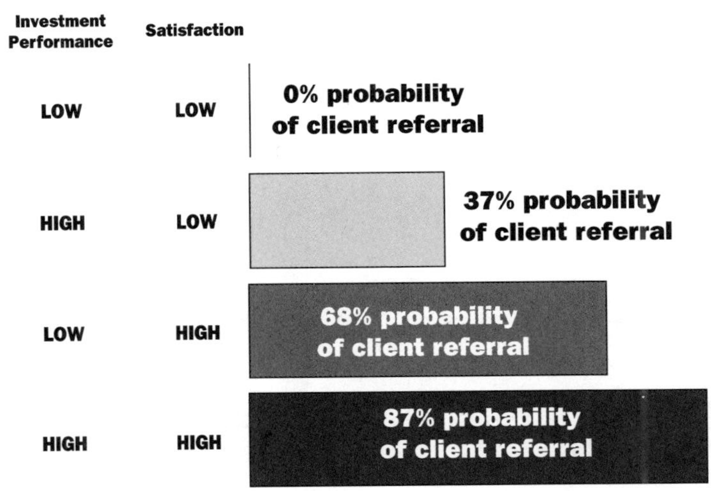

Source: Prince, R.A., and File, K.M. Cultivating the Affluent II: Leveraging High-Net-Worth Client and Advisor Relationships. N.Y.: Institutional Investor, 1997.

There are some clear implications for all investment advisors. For greatest asset capture and greatest client referrals, investment advisors must deliver two benefits to their affluent clients—investment performance and high-quality relationship management. If they do so, their wealthy clients will reward them with incremental assets to manage and with a steady stream of referrals of friends and associates.

It is also good to know that either type of satisfaction — investment performance or interpersonal — can produce positive business building results. It is especially good to know that the one factor over which you have the greatest control — relationship — can build your business even if the market is off.

The Paradigm

When you put all the pieces together, you have the Business Building Model, which is the way to generate highly-satisfied affluent clients (see Exhibit 17.3).

Exhibit 17.3 BUSINESS BUILDING MODELS

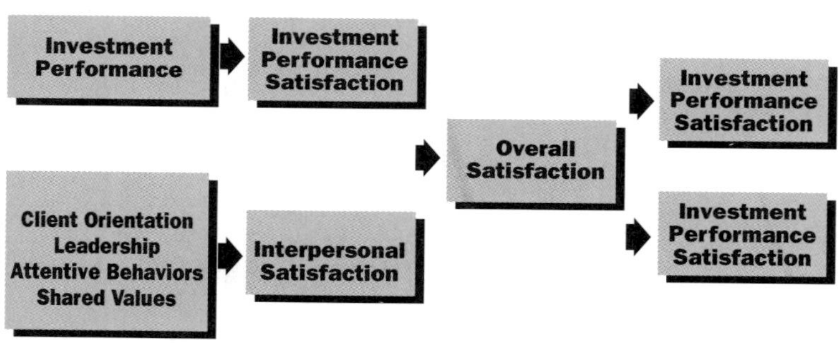

Source: Prince, R.A., and File, K.M. Cultivating the Affluent II: Leveraging High-Net-Worth Client and Advisor Relationships. N.Y.: Institutional Investor, 1997.

If you apply the Business Building Model, you can effectively leverage your affluent client relationships and motivate them to entrust assets as well as refer their family, friends and associates to you. The determining variable in building an investment management business is client satisfaction. That is, the more an affluent client is satisfied with you, the more assets they will entrust to you and the more referrals they will make to you.

The I-CLAS Method for Building Your Business

The I-CLAS method is drawn from Exhibit 17.3 (look at the boxes on the far left). I-CLAS emphasizes relationship management (with four components) compared to investment performance (with one component). Specifically, I-CLAS means:

- **I**nvestment performance.
- **C**lient Orientation.
- **L**eadership.
- **A**ttentive Behavior.
- **S**hared Values.

I-CLAS: Investment Performance

When it comes to achieving all the benefits of loyal affluent clients, investment performance is unquestionably important. No matter how good a job a money manager is doing at relationship management, if poor investment performance keeps happening, the affluent client will ultimately leave — poorer for the experience.

The issue here is client satisfaction with investment performance. Every client will be different. Financial Phobics are more risk-adverse than other personalities, and so they expect (and will be satisfied with) lower returns. Moguls, on the other hand, seek personal wealth and have a higher risk profile. They will want to beat the indices. So your task is to determine the investment performance expectations of each type of investor psychology represented among your clients.

Remember, the deciding factor is high-net-worth client satisfaction. Satisfaction is ultimately a subjective rating system. The only thing that counts is whether affluent clients "feel" their investment portfolio's performance is up to their expectations.

The process of helping wealthy clients get clear about their expectations of performance is an important task. Investment advisors who have excelled in growing their businesses are good at assisting affluent investors define their desired standards of investment performance. What these investment advisors do so well is manage the expectations of their clients as much as they manage their assets. This makes it possible for an affluent client to still be satisfied even when an investment portfolio has performed quite poorly.

What are the strategies that enable investment advisors to manage the expectations of high-net-worth investors? Many of the best of the best focus on the way the assets are to be managed, not on what the end result will be. By concentrating on process (rather than performance) high-performing investment advisors increase their ability to create satisfied affluent clients even if investment performance suffers.

The best investment advisors start the process of managing expectations when they are first introducing their services to affluent prospects. Quite a few use the construct of an investment plan in this process. Institutional clients often have investment plans, individual investors infrequently do. For example, in a survey of 3,724 physicians, only 15.8% had a formally detailed strategy for investing.[8] Investment managers can use the process of creating an investment plan to begin to shape affluent client expectations.

No one can beat the market all the time. Constant superb investment performance is simply beyond the control of most investment advisors. But investment advisors can actively work to manage expectations about investment performance.

I-CLAS: Client Orientation

There is a lot of talk in the investment business about the need to be client-oriented. Investment advisors frequently talk about the need to be client-oriented. However, there is still some confusion in the investment management business about exactly what client-orientation is. We want to take a close look at that actually goes into being client-oriented — from the high-net-worth client's point of view.

When we talk to high-net-worth clients, they have a lot to say about managers who are client-oriented. Clients say they know their investment advisor is client-oriented when they ask a lot of questions, when they feel them out about their needs and when they seem eager to communicate.

Many in-depth interviews with affluent investors enabled us to confirm the exact behaviors that make up client-centered behavior.[9] Client-centered behavior is three behaviors. They are:

- Aggressive time management, so the client has the number of intensity of contacts they want.
- Addressing client needs thoroughly, so clients feel well understood and do not have to explain themselves again.
- Engendering client involvement and participation so clients feel that they own the process.

I-CLAS: Leadership

What affluent investor would not like to work with a leader in the field of money management? Affluent clients are keenly aware they can choose among the best of the best to service their needs. They like to get confirmation that they have picked out the best of the best.

Like all people, they like reinforcement for their decisions. They want reassurance they have made a good decision in selecting their investment advisor. There are a number of concrete ways investment advisors can demonstrate their leadership in the profession, ways that reinforce clients' judgment.

Affluent clients want investment advisors who exhibit the highest standards of leadership in their profession. This does not mean the biggest investment management firm as measured by personnel or even assets under management. It also does not necessarily refer to the firm that might be famous for providing financial services to pension funds or other institutional clients. What they are looking for are leaders in the money management field for affluent investors like themselves.

Keep in mind that the high-net-worth market is a very fragmented market. No one investment manager is in any way a dominant presence. Just consider all the thousands of small boutique money managers and all the financial planners engaged in managing assets for affluent clients. Each and every one of these advisors as well as the larger firms can be recognized as industry leaders by their high-net-worth clients.

In order to achieve the highest ratings of satisfaction from their affluent clients, investment advisors must excel at the interrelated leadership skills of:

- Technical prowess.
- Emphasis on quality.
- Passion for service.

The more an investment advisor can provide testimonial proof of their leadership, the more clients are reassured. We know advisors who write columns, and then mail copies to their client list. We know a few who have hung pictures of their clients' toys to show the fruits of their investments together. Others collect letters from satisfied clients (sometimes you have to ask) and keep them in a portfolio.

Once you start thinking how you can tangibly show your clients your leadership capabilities, you will get ideas that work for you. Remember, you need to demonstrate leadership in ways that will be most influential to the investor personalities of your affluent clients.

I-CLAS: Attentive Behavior

How much time should a money manager spend with a affluent client? This is a business where hand-holding is, for many, a big consumer of time. But how much time should it be? How much is enough? It is too expensive to put in more time than you need, and it can be expensive to ignore wealthy clients.

If your affluent clients frequently have to ask you to call them, or visit them, or send them information, you are not spending enough time with them. If you are not spending enough time with them, your clients are probably dissatisfied. The most satisfied clients do not have to initiate contact with their investment advisors.

The strategic reason to look at the relationship between the number of contacts and satisfaction is that the number of contacts made with individual affluent investors is completely under the investment advisor's control. Unlike soft factors of relationship quality (such as perceived expertise, professionalism and empathy) the number and kind of communications is something you can control with confidence.

Affluent clients demand communications with their investment advisors at the rate of about one every two-and-a-half to three weeks, or between nine and ten such contacts in a six month period. Contacts include fact-to-face visits, telephone conversations and mailed or faxed communications. Interestingly, if the investment manager does not initiate contacts at this rate, affluent clients will initiate it themselves. Thus, between nine and ten contacts per six month period can be considered a benchmark for the industry. Of course, you know by now that investors with different psychologies like different amounts of contact. VIPs like a great deal of contact, as it feeds their esteem needs. Financial Phobics need less, and more reassuring, contacts.

I-CLAS: Shared Values

People like dealing with others who share the same core values. High-net-worth investors are not very different in this regard.

Affluent clients are more satisfied with their interpersonal relationships with their investment advisors if they feel they are similar. However, affluent clients are more concerned that their investment advisors share values, beliefs and standards than share class and lifestyle. What is important is that clients feel they share a basic belief system with their investment advisor.

Fortunately the aspects of one's personality that cannot be changed are least important to affluent investors. The parts of a personality that are good manners and which can be learned by anyone, are the most important to affluent investors. Shared values and personality characteristics explored in research studies include:

- Various aspects of similarity.
- Interpersonal traits.
- Trustworthiness.

Caveat

Investment advisors do a good job of making their affluent clients happy when it comes to the performance of their investment portfolios. How much of this satisfaction is attributable to a rising stock market in the U.S.? What will happen if the markets tumble, as they will likely do one day? Will the investment performance satisfaction ratings tumble as well? They are likely to do so unless the investment advisor is doing a good job of managing expectations and generating high levels of interpersonal satisfaction.

Why don't all investment advisors take the steps to make certain their affluent clients are highly satisfied with the interpersonal nature of their relationship? Maybe they believe it does not matter. Maybe they do not know what those steps are. Maybe it seems too time consuming.

Over many thousands of interviews, we have been able to systematically identify these behaviors the best of the best use to build their businesses. We have been able to help investment advisors build their money management businesses based on these principles. Investment advisors the world over instinctively know about most of these behaviors. But time and time again, we have seen things get in the way of advisors investing the time it takes to develop high-impact client relationships.

To a large degree client relationships are more an issue of acting consistently than taking a huge amount of time. One investment advisory said he did not have the time to do all the unimportant things that would endear him to his clients. However, these unimportant things are what is so important to growing the business, to constructing a $100 million investment advisory practice.

If you truly want to build your business, take the time and take the appropriate initiatives. Investment advisors must consistently behave in ways that build high quality interpersonal relationships. The objective is to be to make these behaviors a habit. When they become a habit, then you will see their tremendous power.

Going Forward

- High-impact client management is behavior that creates client asset capture and client referrals regardless of investment performance.

- Investment performance is important to affluent clients.

- So is a warm personal relationship. Studies show that a good interpersonal relationship can keep a client loyal even if investment performance is off.

- The single most effective business building activity you can do is to achieve both excellent investment performance and excellent relationships. These result in an average of asset capture of $242,000 over two years for each satisfied client and an 87% probability of new client referrals.

- An efficient way to remember the principles of high-impact relationship management is I-CLAS, standing for Investment performance, Client orientation, Leadership, Attentive behavior and Shared values.

$

[1] Prince, R.A., and File, K.M. Cultivating the Affluent II: Leveraging High-Net-Worth Client and Advisor Relationships. N.Y.: Institutional Investor, 1997.

[2] The seven strategic keys are as follows: the competence factor, the hustle factor, the no-surprises factor, the warmth factor, the first-to-know factor, the listening factor and the client-centered factor. These strategic relationship management initiatives are explained in detail in: Prince, R.A., & File, K.M. Cultivating the Affluent: How to Segment and Service the High-Net-Worth Market. New York: Institutional Investor, 1995.

[3] Prince R.A.& File K.M., Marketing to the Affluent: A Toolkit for Life Insurance Professionals. OH: National Underwriter, 1995.

[4] Prince, R.A., and File, K.M. Cultivating the Affluent II: Leveraging High-Net-Worth Client and Advisor Relationships. N.Y.: Institutional Investor, 1997.

[5] ibid.

[6] ibid.

[7] Certainly, affluent investors want good investment performance. However, by critically examining their behavior we know that investment performance is not the real answer. This is especially evident when you take their investor personalities into account.

[8] Prince, R.A., Phillips, E. K., & Apolinsky, H.I. Physician Financial Planning in a Changing Environment. CA: PMIC, 1996.

[9] The use of high-net-worth psychology proves to be extremely helpful in enabling investment advisors to be client-oriented. It provides a template for taking actions that affluent investors will be highly responsive to.

Appendix A

Leveraging Relationships with Affluent Investors for Institutional Investment Management Business

As we have seen, affluent individuals represent an attractive opportunity for independent investment advisors. However, affluent individuals are also a gateway into several institutional investment opportunities.

Opportunity number one is management of retirement assets in mid-sized and smaller companies. The primary source of wealth for affluent individuals in private business ownership. Many independent investment advisors have found they have been able to leverage the confidence of their affluent clients into investment management opportunities for the businesses they own.

Opportunity number two is linked to the charitable interests of the affluent. Many affluent investors are charitably motivated, and find charitable remainder trusts attractive. Opportunities exist to manage the assets under trust. In addition, affluent clients hold leadership positions within many charitable institutions, which have assets in need of investment management.

Opportunity number three exists within that upper tier of the affluent who have created family offices. Investment management opportunities exist in relation to family offices.

A few of the best of the best are already making more from these additional opportunities than they are from fee based investment management services provided to individual affluent clients.

The Retirement Market

Unfunded promises made by Social Security are estimated to be approximately $8 trillion. Because of America's rapidly aging population, it is very unlikely that the same benefits seniors currently get will be available to younger Americans. Some observers have pointed out that those under age 35 are more inclined to believe in UFOs than in ever receiving Social Security benefits. Moreover, the United States is not alone in facing this problem of how to pay for their aging population.[1]

The Opportunity: Affluent Business Owners

The foremost opportunity for the management of retirement assets is in mid-sized and smaller companies.[2] They represent an underpenetrated market. In a study of 4,219 businesses with 300 employees or less, three-quarters (74.8%) did not have a qualified retirement program in place.[3] The overwhelming majority of these smaller and mid-sized firms are privately held as family businesses. Interest in retirement planning among family businesses in considerable.[4]

The mid-sized and smaller companies that want retirement programs for their employees are likely to be the more successful firms. This success tends to translate into owners who, in their own right, may very well require investment advisory services.

As an investment advisor you can position yourself to provide the retirement plan by leveraging your relationship with the affluent business owner. Working from the other direction has also been proven effective. You can position yourself to provide discretionary investment management for the owners and other senior officers of the firm once you are managing their retirement assets.

Because of the public policy crisis over Social Security, the opportunities that exist for investment advisors in the retirement market are enormous. To best capitalize on these opportunities, you need to understand the range of retirement programs that exist[5] as well as be familiar with what is coming down the pike.

(Near) Future Retirement Products

It is likely that new types of retirement products will be created in order to meet the needs and wants of retirement oriented investors. These products will make use of the tax code and combine the latest thinking in portfolio theory coupled with an in-depth understanding of the various segments of investors preparing for retirement.

These products will have a number of characteristics that will make them unique. They will be characterized by operational versatility and will enable the retirement product to solve financial needs that are not (strictly speaking) retirement concerns. Because of their turn-key nature, these products will be available to smaller investors.

These new generation of retirement products plus will be operationally complex as so they will require investment advisors to customize them to investor needs and wants. The investment advisors will be required to not only monitor, evaluate and modify investment decisions, they will also be instrumental in the design phase.

Investment advisors who move quickly as these products are introduced to the retirement market will be best positioned to capitalize on them. While financial institutions will certainly clone such products, the expertise and motivation of investment advisors will be the true determinant of the success of this new generation of retirement products.

The Charitable Market

Investment management needs of the charitable market is growing at an enormous rate. The charitable market can be divided into an affluent segment and an institutional segment.

For the affluent, there is a need for high-quality investment management with respect to charitable trusts. This is a topic which has yet to receive appropriate attention. Specifically, while there is considerable interest by advisors in assisting the will-to-do to establish charitable trusts, there are also extensive pitfalls. For instance, research with wealthy donors shows that most professional advisors lack sufficient technical knowledge. The consequence of these are wealth donors not very satisfied with the experience of creating a charitable trust. And this translates into these donors less inclined to create such gifts in the future.[6]

Aside from the technical knowledge that is essential for case design, what is also required is a detailed understanding of issues surrounding managing the assets in the trust. Because of the fiduciary responsibilities and the liability that accompanies the trust, the investment portfolio in the trust must be appropriately constructed. An extensive review of charitable remainder trusts have shown this is often not the case.[7]

Going beyond charitable trusts to the institutional market we have family foundations. A family foundations is a mechanism by which a well-to-do family can direct their charitable giving. While money management for foundations is technically an institutional business, at this level, we are really dealing with the same psychology as the affluent investor. Even when addressing the larger professionally managed foundations, we are still dealing, to a large degree, with significant aspects of the affluent market. Endowments are another facet of the institutional charitable market that benefits when investment advisors are employed.

All told, the charitable market for investment advisory services is both individual (i.e., charitable trusts and family foundations) as will as institutional (i.e., foundations and endowments). However, even at the institutional level, much of the decision making mirrors the decision making of affluent investors. Why? Because the affluent prove to be especially influential within these institutions.

The Management of Charitable Assets

The primary investment objective of any endowment is the maintenance of the fund, but the maintenance of the spending power of the fund. Thus, not only is a well designed investment strategy required, but it must be complemented with a clearly and properly defined spending strategy.[8]

The trustees must be involved in the key decision making surrounding the investing of the endowments assets. The adoption of well conceived endowment policies insures a long-term orientation that will make results in current as future societal benefits.

In sum, there are basically three objectives that the endowment policy needs to meet:

- Protection of the corpus.
- Stable disbursement of funds.
- Growth of the fund.

In order to achieve these objectives, the real rate of return earned on the assets must exceed the endowments expenditure rate adjusted for inflation. There are a number of general spending policy alternative:

- Expenditures equal to income.
- Expenditures equal to a percentage of assets.

- Expenditures equal to a fixed dollar amount adjusted for inflation.

Which approach is best is a function of the multiple goals and obligations of the endowments. From an investment perspective, it is wise to evaluate all three alternatives.[9]

The Family Office Market

Within the private wealth industry, family offices are categorized as "a collection of affluent investors operating in tandem to maximize their investment return." While in some instances this is true, it tends not to be a fair description of the family office market as a whole. Actually, professionally managed family offices more closely resemble institutional investors than affluent investors.

An affluent family decides it can do a better job geared to the needs and concerns of the family by creating a family office. While the family members are in charge, they hire a financial professional to run the office. What running means, varies from family office to family office. In some cases, it entails making all the decisions, including overseeing the in-house investment management function. In other cases, it means handling the day-to-day chores. Thus, we have a wide spectrum of responsibilities for financial professionals running family offices. Just as it would be a mistake to think for financial institutions to think of all independent investment advisors as alike, it would be a mistake for you to lump all family offices in the same category.

Working with Family Offices[10]

Most heads of family offices embrace the need and desire to preserve and protect their family's fortunes. Other ones are interested in "power," "wealth for its own sake" and "the most advanced investment technology."[11] Family heads of family offices are managing those offices against a specific set of goals. The different profiles provide insights as to the way the offices are to be managed.

Overall, the goal is selection of excellent money managers is the dominant goal irrespective of the profile of the family member. Growing assets is next in importance.

In most cases, the family has considerable influence over some of the decisions of the family office. The great majority of families have at least two family members active as trustees or officers and some have six or more. Family members are also commonly employed by the family office. Furthermore, quite often family members who are not directly involved in the family office have a real say. These family members are shadow influencers.[12]

Based on the research, it is clear that many family offices will be employing more investment advisors in the future. The selection of new investment managers is heavily influenced by family opinion. On the average, more family members get involved in selection decisions than do family office employees. The criteria they use in selecting investment advisors, in many respects, parallels the criteria employed by affluent investors as determined by their psychographic segment.

In sum, affluent investors, in their own right, represent one of the largest and most profitable sources of assets for investment advisors., Their interest in obtaining professional assistance, their relative insensitivity to pricing and performance and the sheer growth in size is the reason they are turning out to be a prime target for a growing number of investment advisors. Recognizing that the personal and professional networks of wealthy investors will lead to an astute investment advisor to institutional money management business, just makes the affluent market all the more attractive.

Implications for Independent Investment Advisors

- For investment advisors, affluent investors are not only rewarding in their own right, they are the way investment advisors can access institutional investment management clients.

- The greatest opportunity in managing retirement assets is among the underpenetrated small and mid-sized businesses. These businesses are predominantly privately held and are mostly family firms.

- The charitable market is replete with the need of investment management expertise. At the individual level there are the assets placed in charitable trusts. Moreover, another underpenetrated market are the small and mid-sized foundations and endowments.

- Family offices are technically prospective institutional clients for investment advisors. At the same time, they exhibit many of the attributes of affluent investors.

[1] Peterson, P.G. Will America Grow Up Before It Grows Old? How the Coming Social Security Crisis Threatens You, Your Family, and Your Country. N.Y.: Random House, 1996.

[2] Hurley, M.P., Meers, S.I., Bornstin, B.J. & Strumingher. The Coming Evolution of the Investment Management Industry: Opportunities and Strategies. N.Y.:Goldman Sachs, 1995.

[3] The study evaluated the reasons for the lack of a qualified retirement program. The conclusions point to the need to have hands-on professionals to educate the business owners as well as work with them in establishing the proper plan and, very importantly, in helping to make investment decisions. The research also points that what these business owners are looking for in retirement products.

[4] Prince, R.A., and File, K.M. Marketing to Family Business Owners: A Toolkit for Life Insurance Professionals. OH: National Underwriter, 1996.

[5] It sometimes seems that investment advisors think only in terms of 401(k) plans. This point of view is not only very much in error, it will prove to be a considerable handicap when competing with more erudite financial advisors. To be most competitive you should be able to implement cross-tested as well as 412(i) plans. As relatively few investment advisors are familiar with these types of retirement plans, you will be at a significant advantage when speaking with business owners of small and mid-sized companies.

[6] Prince, R.A., Rathbun, G.L., & Steiner, C.E. The Charitable Giving Handbook. OH: National Underwriter, 1997.

[7] An examination of 116 charitable remainder trusts found that 42.2% of them had investment portfolios that, presuming they do not produce a return of 20% annually for the life of the trust, will result in the remaindermen receiving nothing. What will the charity then do? Most likely the charity will sue. The charity will sue the trustee(s) of the charitable remainder trust, the investment advisor, the administrator and so forth. Moreover, it is very likely that the charity will win the lawsuit. In order to avoid this very unpleasant situation, the investment portfolio inside the charitable trust should be designed in accordance with the letter and spirit of the charitable trust.

[8] Based on preliminary research, few small and mid-sized endowments are taking all the necessary steps to ensure their endowments are being managed to meet the foundation's or charity's financial needs. This appears to be due to a lack of knowledge on the part of many Trustees. This situation is therefore a golden opportunity for investment advisors. There is enormous

opportunity to educate trustees and consequentially manage endowment and foundation assets.

[9] Small and mid-sized endowments are not making comparative evaluations. This appears to be a significant factor in their less than stellar returns.

[10] This section is based on research conducted by Prince & Associates for Private Asset Management, the newsletter form Institutional Investor. The detailed findings were reported in the newsletter. The survey examined the behavioral pattern of decision making family member in 148 family offices. Each family office was responsible for investing $50 million or more. The nine profiles of wealth psychographic model was the cornerstone of the study.

[11] Family Stewards who constituted more than half the sample. Of the nine segments, only three other segments were represented -- the Moguls, the Accumulators and Innovators.

[12] Prince, R. A., & File, K.M. Marketing to Family Business Owners: A Toolkit for Life Insurance Professionals. OH: National Underwriter, 1996.

Appendix B

About the Authors

Russ Alan Prince

Russ Alan Prince is President of Prince & Associates and is one of the foremost experts on the financial behavior of the affluent. He is an acknowledged expert on the provision of investment and financial services to the global affluent.

His work appears regularly in such specialized publications as Private Asset Manager, National Underwriter, Probe, American Banker, the Chronicle of Philanthropy and Registered Representative. His comments have been reported in Fortune, Forbes, the Wall Street Journal and Business Week.

A prolific writer of academic and trade publication articles, Mr. Prince has co-authored the Seven Faces of Philanthropy: A New Approach to Cultivating Major Donors, the Charitable Estate Planning Process: How to Find and Work With the Philanthropic Affluent, Marketing to the Affluent and Financial Planning for Physicians.

Mr. Prince has a master's degree in sociology from the State University of New York (SUNY) at Stony Brook where he was a Lehman Fellow. He also holds an MBA degree from Columbia University where he was a Dean's Scholar. In 1995, Mr. Prince serves as Expert-in-Residence for the W.K. Kellogg Foundation.

Karen Maru File

Karen File is a managing director of Prince & Associates, the research and consulting firm specializing in financial services for the high-net-worth.

With Russ Alan Prince, Dr. File has co-authored eight books and dozens of articles on marketing financial services to the affluent. Karen File has consulted on aspects of marketing to the wealthy for many institutions.

During the course of her career, she has been a partner at Booz-Allen & Hamilton, a corporate executive and professor of marketing at the University of Connecticut. She holds a Ph.D. in sociology from Temple University and a Masters from Boston University. Her undergraduate training was at Cornell University.

About Prince & Associates

Prince & Associates is a research and consulting firm which specializes in marketing to the high-net-worth investor.

To individual financial and investment advisors, Prince & Associates is a resource for:

- High-net-worth psychology.
- Coaching programs.
- Consulting to high-end producers.

Included among the firm's clients are Oppenheimer, National Life of Vermont, Banker's Trust, The New England, U.S. Trust Company of New York, New York Life, Dean Witter, Mass Mutual and Merrill Lynch. To institutions, Prince & Associates offers:

- Custom marketing and marketing research consulting services.
- The results of syndicated research studies.
- Design and implementation of sales support programs.
- Seminars, workshops, and key-note presentations.